THE SPIRAL OF TIME SERIES

RAV DOVBER PINSON

THE MONTH of SHEVAT

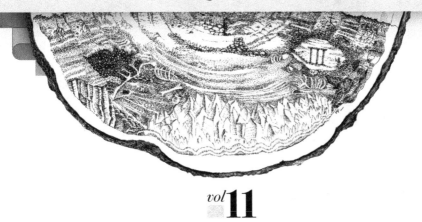

vol **11**

⬥ ELEVATING EATING | TU B'SHEVAT ⬥

IYYUN PUBLISHING

Published by IYYUN Publishing
232 Bergen Street
Brooklyn, NY 11217

http://www.iyyun.com

Iyyun Publishing books may be purchased for educational, business or sales promotional use. For information please contact: contact@IYYUN.com

Editor: Reb Matisyahu Brown

Developmental Editor: Reb Eden Pearlstein

Proofreading: Alyssa Elbogen

Proofreading / Editing: Simcha Finkelstein

Cover and book design: RP Design and Development

Cover image: "Shevat 5776" by Mike Finn @mfinnart
© 2015 Deuteronomy Press, used with publisher's permission as a gift to the Iyyun Center.
See **www.circlecalendar.com** for more information.

pb ISBN 978-0-9914720-6-2

Pinson, DovBer 1971-
The Month of Shevat: Elevated Eating and Tu B'Shevat
1.Judaism 2. Jewish Spirituality 3. General Spirituality

vol **11**

THE MONTH *of* SHEVAT

ELEVATING EATING | TU B'SHEVAT

IYYUN PUBLISHING

DEDICATION

TO

צבי׳ה שתחי׳

MS. HILLARY BARR

In honor of her dear parents

ראובן ומרים (שיחי׳)

MIRIAM & RICHIE FRIEDMAN

and her children

JACLYN MARKOWITZ
גרשונה

STEFANI BERKIN
שרה

WILLIAM (BILLY) BARR
יהושע

ROBERT (ROBBY) BARR
רפאל

CONTENTS

༜

OPENING

ANY CENTURIES AGO, THE SAGES OF ISRAEL were the foremost authority in the fields of both astronomical calculation and astrological wisdom, including the deeper interpretations of the cycles and seasons. Over time, this wisdom became hidden within the esoteric teachings of the Torah, and as a result was known only to students and scholars of the deepest depths of the tradition. More recently, the eminent sage, Rabbi Yitzchak Luria (the Arizal) taught that as the world approaches the Era of Redemption, it is a Mitzvah / spiritual obligation to broadly reveal this wisdom. The decision to disseminate the Torah's previously guarded inner teachings (which reached its apotheosis in the popular revolution of Chasidism that continues to this day) is both a reflection of, and response to, the world's growing spiritual hunger as we wade through the waters of history in the footsteps of Moshiach.

In this spirit, throughout each volume of The Spiral of Time series, we will examine the deeper interpretations and spiritual energies of each of the twelve months of the year. To guide us in this exploration, we will constellate and focus on twelve points of light/information including: a permutation of Hashem's name, a verse from the Torah, a Hebrew letter, the name of the month, a sense or skill, a zodiac sign, a particular tribe of Israel, a body part, a natural element, a series of Torah portions, a season of the year, and the holidays present throughout the month. By reflecting on these twelve themes and categories, we will reveal from within the cycles of time an ever-ascending spiral of insight, understanding, and practical action.

It is our deepest prayer that by spreading and explaining this previously occulted material to the wider public, we will inspire a more profound engagement with the cycles of time we are living through. By learning to navigate and harness the nature of change, as expressed in the spiral of time, we add a sense of deeper purpose and heightened presence to our lives.

In this present volume we will delve into the spiritual nature of the month of Shevat according to these twelve categories.

NOTE: *For a more comprehensive treatment of this twelve-part system and the overarching dynamics of the "story of the year," an in-depth introduction has been provided in Volume One of this series, The Spiral of Time: Unraveling the Yearly Cycle.*

ॐ

The Month of Shevat

THE MONTH OF EXPANSION
& THE ART OF PROPER EATING

ACH MONTH OF THE YEAR ACCORDING TO THE HEBREW calendar radiates with a distinct energy and provides unique opportunities for personal growth and spiritual illumination. Accordingly, each month has a slightly different climate and represents a particular stage in the "story of the year" as expressed through the annual cycles of nature and the history of our people. The winter months call for practices and pursuits that are different than those of the summer months. Some months are filled with holidays, and some have only one or none. Each month therefore has its own natural and spiritual signature.

Shevat is a somewhat peculiar month. It falls decidedly in the winter season, yet it also signals the first stirrings of spring energy and new life. The midpoint of the month, the 15th of Shevat, is a day we celebrate as the "New Year of the Trees," which represents the *awakening of the sap* that has lain dormant all winter. Tu b'Shevat, as this holiday is called, is a ritual acknowledgment of this most subtle of seasonal shifts, the almost imperceptible beginnings of all future blossoming. This dual nature of Shevat — that it is firmly rooted in the dead of winter, while also being connected to the resurrection of spring — provides the key to understanding many of its finer points and illuminating insights.

Simply put: The mental, emotional, and spiritual objective of the month of Shevat is to create healthy relationships with our physical appetites — and most specifically with food. Keep in mind that whenever we mention eating in this volume, it is both literal and symbolic of our relationship with any external object in our lives. Eating is essentially internalizing an object; taking something outside of yourself and ingesting it fully. When we assimilate or consume anything — whether food, information, or imagery — we are integrating its energy into our very being.

As we will explore further, Shevat is an ideal time to focus on our appetites and eating habits. When it is intensely hot during the summer, people tend to eat less. During the colder months, people tend to eat more and bulk up. Yet, paradoxically at the coldest point of the winter, people often lose their appetite; it is simply too cold to eat. This is why Shevat is focused on the Tikkun of eating; as the intensity of the cold begins to weaken and it begins to get slightly warmer, people start to focus on food again. By focusing on refining our appetites and elevating our eating during the month of Shevat, we prepare ourselves for the inevitable challenges that will present themselves in the myriad forms of a beautiful, bountiful world set to break forth in the warmer months ahead.

The task of rectifying our relationship to food and refining our appetites is no easy task. It is a perilous path that takes us to the vulnerable heart of our physicality; a path beset by numerous unconscious obstacles and competing opinions and agendas.

For instance: The instinctive reaction of someone who has a tendency to overeat, or who exhibits any other unhealthy dependency on food, is to abstain from eating — to fast or 'cleanse.' Though effective in the short-term, this quick fix approach is ultimately a form of running away or repression; it therefore does not get to the psycho-spiritual root of one's physical addictions and imbalances. The energy of Shevat, however, provides us with the tools and inspiration to embark upon a far deeper and more developmental approach to correcting these self-sabotaging tendencies — the path of pleasurable engagement with our appetites within the context of holiness and higher consciousness. Once we have secured a healthy relationship to food, we can partake freely; we can eat not only to sustain our bodies, but to experience *Divine Pleasure.* If we learn to enjoy our food with conscious intention and focused attention, we can then taste Hashem's presence within every bite and morsel of food. As a result, we are able to expand the realm of *Kedusha /* holiness and spirituality into the domain of all physical activity — including the sensual experience of taste and the act of eating. As we will see, for a variety of reasons, Shevat is an opportune time for this specific type of spiritual activism.

We will now proceed to explore the inner nature of the month of Shevat based on each of the twelve symbolic categories as discussed above. Each section contributes a piece of the larger puzzle of the month. The effect of integrating the information contained within each section is therefore cumulative. The result is that once one has digested all of the information, so to speak, a far more expansive view of the month comes into sharper focus. This, in turn, empowers each of us to harness the natural/spiritual momentum of each month in order to align our own individual development with the cosmic cycles of nature and the collective stories of our people as articulated in the Calendar.

ϓ

PERMUTATION
OF HASHEM'S NAME

HERE ARE FOUR LETTERS IN THE NAME OF HASHEM (*Yud-Hei-Vav-Hei*) and each month of the year has an inner light that shines through a different permutation of these four letters. Each permutation therefore communicates a different spiritual dynamic encoded within the Divine signature of each particular month. The month of Shevat shines as the combination *Hei-Yud-Vav-Hei*.* It is interesting to note that the only difference between this permutation and the original spelling of the Divine Name is that the sequence of the first two letters is reversed; instead of *Yud-Hei*, it is *Hei-Yud*.

---

*Included with the specific letter permutation of each month is a unique vowel sequence attached to the letters. The vowel sequence for each month is based on the Torah verse for each month, which we will explore shortly. The vowels in the sequence of Hashem's Name for the month of Shevat are *Kamatz –Hei, Sh'va –Yud, Sh'va –Vav, Shuruk –Hei*.

Conceptually, there are two energies present within the month of Shevat. The first half of the month, which lasts from the first of Shevat until the eve of the 15th (Tu b'Shevat), is characterized by *Din* / harshness, constriction, and judgment. This quality of *Din*, as we will see, is an expression of the month's particular permutation of Hashem's Name. The original, natural sequence of the letters of the Name (*Yud* and *Hei*) is an expression of *Chesed* / kindness. However, as brought down in the Zohar, whenever the order of letters in the Divine Name is reversed, this implies an expression of judgment or *Din*. As mentioned, the sequence of the first two letters in the Divine Name is reversed in the month of Shevat: *Hei* then *Yud*, instead of *Yud* then *Hei*. This reversal of the first two letters interrupts the free flow of *Chesed* into the world, and suggests a more constricted flow of Divine energy, which is the quality of *Din*.

On the other hand, the letter combination of the second part of the Divine Name is in its natural flow and sequence: *Vav* then *Hei*. Therefore, the second half of Shevat is much less harsh, and contains more *Chesed*, kindness, and openness (*Ohev Yisrael*, Rosh Chodesh Shevat).

The energetic relationship of moving from harsh judgment to merciful kindness that is encoded in this month's permutation of the Divine Name is also expressed seasonally, as the static winter gives way to the dynamic emergence of new life in the spring. This seasonal shift often registers as one of moving from stuckness or constriction to free-flow and liberation.

As mentioned, the second half of the month begins with the minor holiday of Tu b'Shevat. As the 15th day, Tu b'Shevat is the fulcrum between the two energies of the month and the two halves of the Divine Name — between the *Hei-Yud* and the *Vav-Hei*. As a fulcrum contains the qualities of both sides, so the day of Tu b'Shevat includes all four letters of the Name. Tu means '15,' and 15 is the numerical value of *Yud + Hei*. Shevat is the 11th month of the year (starting from Nisan), and 11 is the numerical value of *Vav + Hei*. Thus, Tu b'Shevat is an expression of the whole Divine Name within a dynamic of *Din* shifting to *Chesed*. On Tu b'Shevat, the natural flow of Divine kindness and compassion is restored.

꠸

TORAH VERSE

ACH MONTH'S REPRESENTATIVE TORAH VERSE IS CON-
NECTED to its unique Divine signature. The permutation of the letters in the Divine Name specific to each
month, provides an acronym for each month's particular verse. Additionally, the vowels attached to the acronymic letters in the Torah
verse of the month are combined with the month's permutation of
G-d's Name, as mentioned in a note above. The verse of the month
of Shevat is found in the book of *Vayikra*: *Hamer Yemirenu V'ha-
ya Hu...*/ If anyone makes a substitution, both the animal [and
its substitute become holy] (27:33). This verse teaches us that if a
person who has selected an animal for Temple Sacrifice decides to
exchange his designated animal for a different one, both animals
are then considered holy. In such a *Temurah* / exchange, one must
receive something equal in value to what they have offered: the
two objects must be, in a sense, the same. Previously, however, one

object was holy and the other was not; but now, to create an equal exchange, they are both holy. This is an expansion of *Kedusha* or holiness into new territory, so to speak. Like the flame of a candle that can light the wick of other candles without losing any of its own fire, Kedusha can expand or transfer from one source to another without diminishment. In reality, sharing and spreading the light only serves to dispel more darkness.

The concept of *Temurah* is related to the concept of *Targum* / translation; specifically Moshe's translation of the Torah from the Holy Tongue into the 70 root languages of the secular world. This exchange or transfer of Torah from one language to another elevated each secular language into the realm of holiness, and the previously narrow boundary of holiness was thereby expanded to embrace and include seemingly mundane aspects of life. From then on, whenever people study Torah in a language other than Hebrew, that linguistic expression is included within the holiness of the revelation of Mount Sinai. Appropriately, Moshe translated the Torah into the 70 languages on Rosh Chodesh Shevat, the month that gives us the power to expand the borders of Kedusha into the realm of what was once considered mundane.

In Shevat, this principle of exchanging and expanding holiness applies specifically to eating — a basic physical necessity which we share with all of life. A complete Tzadik / a righteous or enlightened person can taste the Divinity within the physical food they eat. For such a person, the physical pleasure of the food is an exchange or expansion of the Divine vibration that gives rise to the food. In other words, the outer form of the food becomes equal to the Divine vibration within it; the physicality of the food becomes spiritualized. Tasting Divinity is one way a Tzadik expands Kedusha into the realm of eating.

Everyone can expand holiness in this way, to some extent. This is because the pleasure we experience when we eat does not ultimately come from the physicality of the food. It comes from the spiritual word of Hashem vibrating within the food, as it is written: "For not by bread alone will man live, but by the word of Hashem…" (*Devarim*, 8:3. *Likutei Torah* (*Arizal*) ad loc. *Baal Shem Tov al haTorah, Ekev*, 2). Our task during the month of Shevat is to focus on the *spiritual taste* within the food we eat, and thereby expand or translate holiness into the realm of physical pleasure. We will continue to revisit and explore this idea of tasting the Divine vibration within our food throughout the following pages of this text.

☾

🜔

LETTER

*T*HE HEBREW LETTER ASSOCIATED WITH SHEVAT IS TZADI, צ.The name of this letter is popularly pronounced *Tza-dik*, meaning a righteous or enlightened person (*Shabbos*, 104a; further expounded in the *Medrash*, *Osiyos d'Rebi Akiva*). A Tzadik is defined by, among other things, his relationship to food; as this basic physical appetite is one of the foundations upon which the edifice of one's psyche is initially erected and ultimately rectified. The Torah says that for a Tzadik, eating is inherently satisfying: "The *Tzadik* eats to satisfy his soul; but the belly of the *Rasha* / one who willfully invests his life-force in self-centered indulgence for its own sake is always empty" (*Mishlei*, 13:25).*

---

* "*Eliyahu HaNavi* once said to *Rav Nason*: Eat a third and drink a third and leave a third for when you get angry, and then you will have had your fill" (*Gittin*, 70a). This approach to eating is only valid for people who get angry. Those who are humble and less prone to anger can eat until they are full (*Degel Machena Ephrayim, Bechukasai*). As the *Pasuk* says: "The humble shall eat and be full" (*Tehillim*, 22:27). As it says, "The Tzadik eats to satisfy his soul; but the belly of the wicked is always empty" (*Mishlei* 13:25). This is the highest form of eating: to eat from a state of spiritual fullness, and until one is physically full.

The Tzadik eats mindfully and for a clear purpose: nourishment of the body. Although a Tzadik's food choices may tend to be more nourishing and healthy than those of a less illuminated person, it is primarily the purposefulness of the Tzadik's eating that brings real satisfaction. According to the Zohar: "The Tzadik eats for satisfaction" means that the Tzadik eats *from a place of* satisfaction (*Zohar 2, Beshalach*, 62b). In other words: the Tzadik is already satisfied — from his prayer, study, meditation, and acts of generosity — before he or she even begins eating. Therefore, the Tzadik eats from a state of spiritual wholeness and fulfilment, not from a place of existential lack. This experience of lack leads one to eat for all kinds of reasons other than nourishing their body, as we will now explore.

Often, people eat to compensate for some uncomfortable emotion or psycho-spiritual hunger. There is a *Cheser* / lack and they eat to fill this inner emptiness. People eat and overeat when they are feeling dejected and crave comfort food, or when they are feeling lonely and crave external stimuli. People who are nervous may eat to calm themselves down, as the repetitive act of chewing can calm the nerves. There are also people who feel the need to eat and fill themselves up after undergoing a deeper spiritual experience such as prayer or study. All of these types of eating are, for the most part, unhealthy and ultimately counterproductive; in the end, "the belly [still] feels empty." A Tzadik, on the other hand, is one who doesn't eat to fill an emotional need, but eats simply to feed the body so that he or she can have the strength to serve Hashem (*Medrash Rabbah, Vayikra* 34. *Tanya*, Chap. 29). Thus, a Tzadik eats the right amount of food at the right time, and feels equally satisfied before, during, and after eating.

Although a Tzadik is not attached to the physical pleasure of taste, he or she is able to enjoy the presence of the Divine within and through that pleasure. As stated, the Tzadik is already 'full' — there is no lack, neediness, or attachment in their relationship to food. Yet, from this place of non-attachment, they choose to partake in the physical pleasure of the food in order to enjoy the presence of the Divine within it.

On the other hand, a person who believes that fullness or satisfaction comes from an external object, in our case food, may eat the same amount or same kind of food as the Tzadik; but since he eats in a mindless and misdirected way, his eating only exacerbates his physical, emotional, and spiritual hungers.

What exactly does it mean to exchange the pleasure of the world for Divine pleasure? And, how do we do this?

The Prophet exclaims, "The whole earth is full of His glory" (*Yeshayahu*, 6:3). This is a powerful and poetic statement that can be interpreted in two ways: a) Hashem's glory fills the entire world, and b) the fullness of the world (i.e., the beauty, majesty, and wonder of the world) is Hashem's glory.

The latter interpretation provides us with an illuminating lens through which to view and engage Hashem's glory in the world. When we take a delicious apple in our hand, we can stop for a moment and appreciate its shape, beauty, texture, and color. We can take another moment and acknowledge the wondrous workings of nature that led up to our holding the apple: the seed that settled into the soil; the rain that fell and irrigated the tree; the sun that shined and gave nutrients to the tree; the amount of time the little sapling took to grow into an adult tree; and the precise weather, climate, and other conditions (including human input and ingenuity) that allowed this fruit to become edible and available to us. Then, when you recite a blessing thanking the Creator for this truly miraculous creation, take a bite and relish in the taste, you are truly having an embodied spiritual experience. In this little bite of fruit, you are encountering the tangible majesty of Creation itself. In this way, the fullness of Creation can serve to awaken your appreciation of the glory of the Creator.

As explained, Shevat empowers us to expand the borders of Kedusha to embrace our seemingly mundane and physical world. This is illustrated by the Torah verse of the month explored above, by Moshe's translation of the Torah into the 70 languages on the first of Shevat, by the practice of eating like a Tzadik, and by recognizing Hashem's glory in the food that you eat.

The first time the letter Tzadik appears in the Torah as the first letter of a word,* it is in the word *Tzon* / sheep (*Bereishis*, 4:2). *Tzon* comes from the word *Tzei* / to go out, as the nature of sheep is to go out into the open fields in order to graze and roam freely. This signifies the idea of elevating the sparks in the 'outer' fields of reality — thereby expanding the spiritual sphere of Kedusha in order to incorporate and elevate the physical realm.

---

* It is brought down in the name of the Vilna Gaon that the first time a letter appears as the beginning of a word in the Torah signifies the underlying energy of that particular letter (*Toldos Yitzchok* by a *Talmid* of *Rav Isaac Chover*, p. 39b. See also *Bnei Yissachar, Iyyar, Maamar* 3). There is a source for this in the *Gemara*. The *Gemara* (*Baba Kama*, 55a) says that if someone sees the letter *Tes* in his dream it is a good sign. Although there are other words in the Torah that begin with *Tes* (some good, some not so good), it is still considered to be a good sign because the first time *Tes* appears in the Torah is at the beginning of the word *Tov* / good (*Bereishis*, 1:4).

As mentioned previously, the technically correct way to pronounce the letter of the month is *Tzadi*, which means hunt. The idea of hunting also implies an expansion of holiness, as we must track and capture the holy sparks and return them to the fold of Kedusha — the original, integral state of all Creation.

ঙ্গ

NAME OF THE MONTH

HE WORD SHEVAT MEANS ROD OR STAFF, SUGGESTING hitting and harshness. During this month, we read in the Torah about the Ten Plagues that befell the Egyptians in the story of the Exodus. Our Sages call these plagues the *Makos* / hits. These harsh judgments were channeled through the *Sheivet* / staff of Moshe.

Moshe found this miraculous staff in the garden of *Yisro*, and realized that it was the very staff that was created at the beginning of time, during the twilight of the Sixth Day of Creation, right before Shabbos. The Four Letter Name of Hashem was inscribed on this staff (*Targum Yonason, Shemos*, 2:21). When Moshe held the staff in its upright position, the Name of Hashem was arranged in the natural order and thus brought down Divine *Chesed* / kindness to the People of Israel and to the world. When, however, he would turn the staff upside-down, then the Name of Hashem appeared in reverse order, which channeled an energy of Divine *Din* / harsh judgement into the world. When Hashem desired to push Egypt to expel the People of Israel, Moshe turned the staff upside-down, and the *Makos* ensued. This is the deeper reason why Hashem tells Moshe to "take his staff" (*Shemos*, 7:19, 8:1), or to "lift his staff" (*Shemos*, 14:16), when He wanted to reveal another miraculous *Maka* through him in Egypt. For when Moshe takes up and turns over the staff, the order of the Divine Name is reversed and harsh judgment is brought into the world.

According to some *Medrashic* sources, each plague lasted one week. According to this count, the first of the Ten Plagues occurred ten weeks before *Pesach*, the Exodus from Egypt, which is the beginning of the month of Shevat (*Pesikta Zutra, Parshas Bo*, 24). However, most *Medrashic* sources speak of each of the Ten Plagues lasting a full month, except for the tenth plague, which lasted one night (*Medrash Rabbah* and *Tanchuma*, ad loc). According to this view, it is possible that the first of the Ten Plagues began in the month of Tamuz, nine months before Nisan, and that the last three or four plagues, which were the harshest group, began in Shevat.

In the numerological system of *Mispar Katan* / small numbers, the value of the word Shevat is 14 (*Shin*/3 + *Beis*/2 + *Tes*/9 = 14). As explored earlier, the *Din* / harshness of Shevat is manifest primarily during the first 14 days of the month. From Tu b'Shevat / the 15th of Shevat to the end of the month, the attribute of *Chesed* / Divine kindness and giving is dominant.

The full numerical value of the three letters of the word Shevat is 314 (*Shin*/300 + *Beis*/2 + *Tes*/9 + 3/for the three letters = 314). This is the same numerical value as the Divine Name, *Shad-dai* (*Ma'or vaShemesh*, Rimzei Tu b'Shevat). The name *Shad-dai* is related to three Hebrew words: a) *Shoded* / break or destroy — hinting at the element of *Din* / judgment and restriction; b) *Shadayim* / the bosom which nourishes an infant (*Shir haShirim*, 8:1. *Noam Elimelech*, Vaera) — hinting at the idea of food; and c) *Sh'dai* / enough. Our Sages teach: As the world was being created, it was expanding endlessly, until Hashem said to the world, "*Sh'dai* / enough!" (*Chagigah*, 12a).

The first half of Shevat relates to the aspect of *Shoded* and Din. At the end of the 14th day, a force appears, so-to-speak, that says, "*Sh'dai* — enough harshness!" If we heed this call by making a *Tikkun* in our relationship to food, then the rest of our month is full of *Chesed*, like the kindness and love of a mother nourishing her beloved baby.

As mentioned, the first time a letter appears in the beginning of a word in the Torah is directly representative of the underlying energy of that particular letter. In the Torah, the first words to begin with the letters *Shin*, *Beis*, and *Tes* respectively (the letters of the word Shevat) are the following:

Shin — *Shamayim* / Heaven

Beis — *B'reishis* / In (or *for*) the beginning. The word *Reishis* alludes to *Chochmah* / wisdom, as in the verse "*Reishis Chochmah*..." (*Tehillim*, 111:10. *Targum Yerushalmi, Bereishis*, 1:1)

Tes — *Tov* / good

In order to create and stimulate a proper *Birur Nitzutzos* / identification and elevation of the holy sparks within a certain object, we need to first look for the *Reishis*, the original wisdom present within that thing. Once we have found the point of Divine wisdom within that particular thing, including what we can learn from the object and how the object can be used to serve a higher purpose, we can then perceive the *Tov*, the true nature of goodness within the object. With practice, we will eventually be able to locate and connect to the inherent wisdom and goodness within each and every creation, thereby elevating its spark to its root in *Shamayim* / Heaven.

The month of Shevat is like a rod with which we can break open the *Kelipa* / shell that conceals the spiritual nature of the food we eat, revealing the Divine wisdom and holy sparks within it. Every time we eat, we have an opportunity to elevate sparks of holiness. Even on a physical level, when we are grinding food with our teeth — sifting out the nourishment from the inert matter, processing and absorbing the nutrients, and eliminating the waste — we are potentially elevating the dormant sparks of holiness. The key to this redemptive process is conscious intention, focused attention, and awareness of higher potential.

The word Shevat (*Shin-Beis-Tes*) is also related to the word Shabbos (*Shin-Beis-Tav*, also pronounced *ShaBaT*). Since the two letters *Tes* and *Tav* are both lingual consonants, they are considered interchangeable. (This is a traditional and accepted form of oral letter permutation for the purposes of creative interpretation.) Additionally, according to many sources, the name Shevat is adapted from the Akkadian (Assyrian-Babylonian) name for the eleventh month of the year: *Shabatu.*

On the day of Shabbos, we enjoy eating in complete holiness, as the flow of Kedusha permeates all of Creation without obstruction. On Shabbos, the physical world is a completely transparent vessel of spiritual reality. Furthermore, the Arizal teaches that on Shabbos there is no waste. This means that everything can be integrated and elevated, and thus everything is permeated with holiness. A *Talmid Chacham* / wise student of Torah is called Shabbos (*Zohar* 3, 29a). By extension, a Tzadik who embodies the spirit of Shabbos can eat in holiness, with no waste, on every day of the week.

Aside from its mystical application, wherein a human being consumes food and absorbs it completely without dispelling any of it, this idea can also refer to a level of awareness that recognizes the purpose and therefore the goodness of everything — including waste matter. This transforms the very idea of waste itself into something more generative and useful. According to this perspective: *nothing is ever wasted, as everything serves a higher purpose.*

♉

SENSE

*A*CCORDING TO THE EARLY AND ENIGMATIC TEXT known as the *Sefer Yetzirah*, the *Chush* / sense connected with Shevat is *Le'itah* / taste. The verse in *Tehillim* / Psalms (34:9) says, *Ta'amu uRi'u Ki Tov* Hashem / Taste and see that Hashem is good. Reb *Elimelech* of Lizhensk, the legendary Chassidic Tzadik, interprets this verse to mean: Taste and see that all goodness is in fact Hashem. Living in this state of consciousness, the pleasurable tastes of food are no longer experienced as mundane or merely self-serving; they are holy in and of themselves, for through them we can taste Hashem's presence and Infinite majesty within every finite morsel of food.

The word *Ta'am* / taste can be viewed as an acronym for the three fundamental reasons why we engage with life: because it is *Tov* / good, *A'rev* / sweet, and *Mo'il* / beneficial (see; *Sedei Eliyahu, Berachos*, 8a. *Pirush haGra, Mishlei*, 17:24. 10:2. *Shaloh HaKodesh, Sha'ar HaOysyos, Oys* 10). All the goodness, sweetness, and benefit for us in this world are from the Creator and part of the Creator's goodness and sweetness. Seen from this perspective: the realm of spirituality, when activated with the proper intention, discipline, and perspective, is ultimately meant to be expanded to embrace the pleasurable world of physicality.

Eating 'for the sake of Heaven' — for the purpose of strengthening ourselves for contemplative prayer, Torah study, or righteous actions — is a very high practice. This way of eating is, in a sense, a Mitzvah. If, for example, a person sleeps well at night so that they will have strength to study Torah the next day, their sleep becomes joined to the Mitzvah of Torah study (*Mordechai, Sukkah*, 26a, *Oys* 740). And yet, this is still only a means to an end; it is part of the Mitzvah but it is not the Mitzvah of Torah study itself.

There is a way of living, however, that is even deeper than acting 'for the sake of Heaven.' Rather than acting for the sake of something else (even Heaven), our actions can be holy in and of themselves (*Rambam, Hilchos De'os*, 3:2-3. *Likutei Sichos*, 10: 104-105). This is the implication of a powerful verse in Proverbs: *b'Chol Derachecha Da'eihu* / Know Hashem in all your ways (*Mishlei*, 3:6). "This is a very small verse," say our Sages, "but the entire Torah is connected to it" (*Berachos*, 63a). That is, everything that you do — not just the official Mitzvos, but even eating, sleeping, procreation, and working — is a potential way of knowing Hashem.

'To know' means to be intimate. Intimacy and closeness with Hashem in everything we do is the ultimate pleasure we can experience. *Oneg* / pure pleasure, is the opposite of *Nega* / affliction. There is nothing higher than *Oneg* and nothing lower than *Nega* (*Sefer Yetzirah*). *Nega* comes about through acts of *Pirud* / separation, such as speaking *Lashon haRa* / negative or separative speech (*Erachin*, 16a). As a consequence of speaking *Lashon haRa*, the speaker must spend time *Badad* / alone, isolated from the community, to realize the extent of the affliction caused by their words.

Oneg, on the other hand, is the collapse of self within something else. The *Oneg* of food or music is not when you are aware of being a separate self who is enjoying the specific tastes or sounds, but rather when you lose yourself completely within the experience itself. For example, in marital intimacy, the ultimate bliss of the partners is achieved when they merge completely and lose consciousness of being separate selves. Pure pleasure is thus found in *Yichud* / unity.

However, the physical objects and experiences that give us pleasure in this world are limited and finite. When finite ears are enjoying finite music, there is still a limited self that is experiencing something outside of itself. If we do succeed in losing ourselves in a finite experience, it is fleeting and superficial, and so abiding pure pleasure is not accessed. Only by losing our entire selves in the Infinite Source of all life, from which all finite phenomena flow, and actively living in unison with this Source, can we experience the perpetual peak of all pleasure.

In the teachings of the Arizal there are many *Kavanos* / intentions and practices of *Yichudim* / unifications connected to the various Mitzvos. The new path opened up in the teachings of the Baal Shem Tov is that these Kavanos are extended into all human activities, not merely those that are overtly sacred (*Toldos Yaakov Yoseph, Bo*). This is also called the *Avodah* / spiritual work within *Gashmiyus* / physicality. In everything we do, we have the ability to elevate sparks and connect to the deeper reality within the physical acts and objects involved. Even in the simple act of eating food a person can create the most wonderful *Yichudim* / unifications between Heaven and Earth (*Toldos Yaakov Yoseph, Va'eira*).

With deep wisdom and a profound understanding of life, we can learn to see more clearly into every action we perform and every situation we experience. "By putting our heart and soul [into what we are experiencing,] we are able to see and hear the Divinity and wisdom that is hidden within all levels of existence" (*Ohr haMeir, Rimzei Koheles*, p. 313). Furthermore, "When a person is able to look at everything and acknowledge the *Kavod* / honor or glory of the Creator within it, he creates a unity between himself and the *Kevod Hashem* and thus elevates the object or activity with which he is involved" (*Ma'or Einayim, Likutim, Yishayahu*, 40:26).

In the month of Shevat, we focus on elevating our eating so that it should be mindful, deliberate, wise, and purpose-filled, rather than unconscious, careless, or emotionally driven. Once we are able to eat for the sake of gaining strength for prayer, Torah study, Mitzvos and good deeds, rather than to fill some psycho-emotional lack or imbalance, then we can step into an even higher level: to seek to *know* Hashem intimately and pleasurably in all our ways. We can then begin to extend Kedusha into all aspects of our life.

☾

♈

SIGN

THE HEBREW ASTROLOGICAL SIGN OF SHEVAT IS *D'li* / THE Pitcher, corresponding to Aquarius, the Water-Bearer or Water-Pourer. The word *D'li* comes from a root which means "to lift up" (*Tehillim*, 30:2). As we will see, this idea connects with the act of expanding the realm of Kedusha into the seemingly mundane in order to elevate the fallen sparks hidden within all aspects of creation.

Aquarians are known as idealists who yearn to expand beyond or break down boundaries. Aquarians tend to ask unsettling questions, rebel, start revolutions, and seek out what is fresh and exciting. They are often cultural creatives. They seek to expand the Torah's teachings of justice and righteousness to all. In essence, this is a profoundly positive and even Messianic inclination. On the other hand, the shadow side of this focus is that instead of working on changing themselves, they prefer to focus only on changing society at large — which often backfires for lack of addressing the inner, personal roots of the world's social issues. In their caring for the world, which at its root is a righteous inclination, they may unwittingly cultivate a blind-spot for their own inner turmoil, including their immediate family and community. When an Aquarian personality connects to the wisdom of the Torah, however, this blind-spot can be rectified.

An early Biblical commentator known as the *Even Ezra* (on *Shemos*, 31:18. Rabbi *Hai Gaon*, *Sefer Yetzirah* 4:2) and the later Chassidic Rebbe, the *Bnei Yissachar* (*Shevat*), both explain that the Jewish People as a whole are most influenced by the constellation of Aquarius. The letter *Tzadik*, which, as mentioned before, is the letter of the month, is also especially connected with the people of Israel (*Ra'avad*, *Sefer Yetzirah*, 2:3; *Toras Nasan*, *Vayishlach*). On the surface, these teachings seem to contradict an important principle stated by our Sages, that *Ein Mazal l'Yisrael* / There is no constellation for Israel (*Shabbos*, 156b, according to one opinion; *Nedarim*, 32a) — meaning that astrology has no influence over the people of Israel. More accurately, this statement means that when we connect deeply with the infinite light of Torah, we are able to transcend any and all pre-determined or fixed finite limitations — including astrological influences (*Even Ezra*, *Devarim*, 4:19; *Ohr haChayim*, *Bechukosai*). When we do so, then from a place *above astrology*, we can utilize astrological energies for holy purposes.

This is the essence of the Jewish People's association with the constellation of Aquarius: As a *D'li* or pitcher is used to pour water, so too we can pour the water of Torah for others, and quench the spiritual thirst of all who are receptive. But we can only do this if we work on refining ourselves to access our inner *Tzadik*. This is one way that we can utilize the energy of Aquarian idealism to expand *Kedusha* into the whole world.

Eliezer, the loyal servant of Avraham, was called the *Demeshek*, literally 'the one from Damascus.' *Medrashically*, the word *Demeshek* means *Doleh u-Maskeh* / he pours and gives over the teachings of his master *Avraham*. In the acrostic method of interpretation, this phrase can be read as *Doleh* / he drew, *u-Mashke* / and gave to drink (*Yumah*, 28b. *Rashi*, Bereishis 15:2). In any case, the energy of *D'li* teaches us to work hard on ourselves in order to expand holiness by giving over Torah wisdom to others — satisfying the thirst of their souls with Divine teachings.

TRIBE

*A*sher IS THE ISRAELITE TRIBE CORRESPONDING to the month of Shevat. The letters of the name *Asher* (*Alef-Shin-Reish*) can be rearranged to form the word *Rosh* / head. Shevat contains the *Rosh haShanah* / New Year of the trees (according to different opinions, this falls on either the 1st or the 15th day of the month). The letters of Asher can also be reversed to form an acronym: *Rosh Shenos Ilanos* / The Rosh haShanah of the Trees.

What does the Tribe of Asher represent? The Torah says, "As for Asher, fat (rich, delicious) is his produce" (*Bereishis*, 49:20). This means Asher is associated with the essence of *Ta'anug* / pleasure and the enjoyment of fatty, tasty foods (*Pri Tzadik*, Shevat).

Asher is also associated with oil, which is a dominant theme in both the blessing that his father Yaakov gave to him as well as the blessing that Moshe gave to the Tribe of Asher before entering into the Holy Land. Yaakov's final blessing for Asher is that his territory in the Land of Israel (north of modern Haifa) should produce an abundance of olives, which will be pressed into olive oil (*Bereishis*, 47-50). Similarly, at the end of his life, Moshe blessed the Tribe of Asher: "...The most blessed of children is Asher. He shall be pleasing to his brothers, and dip his feet in oil" (*Devarim*, 33:24). Among many other things, oil alludes to fatty, luscious foods, which are rooted in the realm of *Ta'anug* / pleasure.

The name Asher shares a root with the word *Ashirus* / affluence. Delicious and delicate-foods such as fruit represent affluence since they are not usually considered basic staples, like bread and water. They are eaten more for flavor and enjoyment rather than for survival. Therefore, on Tu b'Shevat the custom is to taste a royal array of exotic and delicious fruits, in resonance with the affluent energy of the month (*Magen Avraham, Orach Chayim*, 131: 16, in the name of the *Tikkun Yissachar*, p. 22b). Additionally, the Lubavitcher Rebbe of blessed memory, enacted a custom to specifically eat fruit from the Land of Israel on the 15th day of Shevat.

Fruits and trees, more than vegetables and shrubs, are connected to the realm of Pleasure and to a *world beyond necessity*. Adam/

Humanity 'shrunk' after eating from The Tree of Knowledge (*Medrash Rabbah, Bereishis*, 12: 6. See also *Sanhedrin*, 38b), meaning that he was demoted in spiritual stature. The same thing occurred with the 'Wheat Tree' that he ate from. (According to some *Medrashim*, the fruit eaten by *Chava* and *Adam* in the Garden was actually wheat.) Before this catastrophic eating, wheat grew tall and upright like a tree. Afterwards, the stature of the plant was 'diminished' and it began to grow nearer to the ground (*Medrash Rabbah, Bereishis*, 15:7). The wheat 'tree' was thus demoted to a grain. Trees and the fruit that grow upon them are therefore still connected to the primordial world of Pleasure, represented by the Tree of Life, as will be explored shortly.

Asher is also related to the words *Ashur* and *Ashrei* / fortunate, alluding to the exalted Sefira of Keser / Crown, which represents the Divine attribute of Holy Desire and Pleasure. Keser signifies the realm of Unity as a crown covers, and thus includes, the entire body below, integrating all of its separate parts within a single sphere. In the nondual realm of Keser, everything is unified and equal, and yet this is precisely where one experiences the ultimate *Ta'anug* or *Oneg*.

From this we understand that the foundation of pure and holy pleasure is selfless equanimity. When all tastes are theoretically equal before us and we have the freedom of detachment, then we can delight and relish in all of the earth's abundant delights without being harmed, sucked in, or swallowed up by them. Rabbi *Yehudah haNasi*, the great Second Century sage, lived on this level. Although his home was full of the richest foods and delicacies, which he certainly enjoyed, at the end of his life he honestly proclaimed: "I did not partake in the pleasures of this world, not even in the measure of a small finger" (*Kesuvos*, 104a. *Likutei Sichos*, 31. p. 176, note 61).

The practice of equanimity in relation to food is first revealed in Genesis, where Hashem tells Adam and Chavah / Eve, "From every tree of the Garden you may eat, but from the Tree of the Knowledge of Good and Evil you must not eat..." (*Bereishis* 2:16-17). Adam and Chavah are living in Paradise where there is no duality or opposites, and they are told that they should not eat from the Tree of Duality. This is the simple reading, and is most commonly understood to imply that there are two separate trees, the Tree of Life and the Tree of Knowledge.

However, from a deeper perspective, the passage implies that there is really only one all-inclusive reality, which includes "all trees" (*Pri Tzadik*, Tu b'Shevat). Therefore, Hashem is saying, "You may eat freely from *every* tree — alluding to the Tree of Life — but do not eat from *one specific* tree and exclude other trees, because then you will enter into the paradigm of the Tree of Duality" (*Ma'or vaShemesh*, *Parshas Bo*, p.179-180). Put more simply, Hashem is saying that: *you may eat 'everything,' just not 'something.'* If you eat from every tree equally and do not make exclusive distinctions, it will all feel and taste the same. In this state of consciousness, even the non-fruit parts of the tree will then taste like fruit (*Medrash Rabbah*, *Bereishis*, 5:9). The moment we embrace one kind of feeling or experience and reject another, we move away from equanimity and enter the world of duality, where one thing is good and another is not. In truth, all is from Hashem; this is the perspective of the Tree of Life.

We will explore this theme of equanimity much more thorough-
ly later on in our text. For now suffice it to say that equanimity is
an extremely important attribute for one to develop, although it
is not the highest level of spiritual attainment. As we said earlier,
equanimity is the *foundation* of pure and holy pleasure, which we
will learn is beyond mere detachment or disinterest.

BODY PART

ACCORDING TO MANY COMMENTATORS, THE body part connected to the month of Shevat is the *Kurkavan* / esophagus (others translate it as stomach). The *Kurkavan* grinds or helps process our food (*Berachos*, 61b). As we have learned, the inner energy of the month of Shevat impels us to rectify our relationship to eating and processing food.

One way that Shevat helps us to do this is by encouraging us to explore the physical, psychological, and spiritual effects of an empty stomach. All of the weeks of Shevat are part of a period called *ShoVaViYM*, which is a six-week period (and during a leap year, *ShoVaViYM TaT,* an eight week period), in which fasting is frequently prescribed by the Kabbalists. *ShoVaViYM* and *ShoVaVi-YM TaT* are acronyms for the six or eight Torah portions that are read during this period, starting with *Shemos.* Fasting from physical food allows us to become more aware of our relationship to eating. Are we in the habit of eating for the sake of superficial pleasure? Do we depend on food for psychological and emotional comfort? When we return to eating after fasting, can we focus on the deeper, spiritual realities within our food, or do we go right back to where we were before we fasted, eating unconsciously and impulsively?

This is the message of Shevat: If we would take the time to contemplate the spiritual significance of what food really is, and what eating represents and reveals about the state of our soul, we would be careful to eat with greater appreciation and increased mindfulness. Eating in such an exalted manner actually has the power to diminish *Din* in our lives, and restore the flow of *Chesed* in the world by recognizing and tapping into the Divine presence within all aspects of our life — even the most physical and seemingly mundane. As a result, we can experience true pleasure, which is the awareness and experience of Hashem's presence in every aspect of our lives.

Our Sages teach us about a certain *Kohen* who ate large amounts of food, yet his eating was done in holiness (*Pesachim,* 57a). Holy eating has less to do with the amount we eat, and is more connected to the way we eat — whether or not we are coming from a place of satisfaction or lack. Holy eating is eating with purpose and presence, plain and simple.

ELEMENT

S HEVAT CORRESPONDS TO THE ELEMENT OF *Avir* / AIR or *Ruach* / wind. The gift of air is flexibility and mobility. Those connected with this element are good communicators and interpreters. The other months associated with wind are Sivan and Tishrei. In both of those two months, we received the preeminent Divine communication from Above, the Torah. The first set of *Luchos* / Tablets was given to us during the month of Sivan, and the second set of Luchos during Tishrei, on Yom Kippur. In the month of Shevat there is an even deeper transmission of Torah, as it is the month when Moshe began to translate the Torah into the 70 root languages of the world, as discussed above. This flawless translation by Moshe is the seed of the dissemination of Torah to all Creation. This is the ultimate communication of Torah, which had — and has — the power to alter the way the entire world perceives reality. The message of Shevat is one of radical inclusivity. Not only those who stood at Mount Sinai are privy to Hashem's word and love; now, all people of all languages can potentially comprehend the Unity of Hashem and potentially return to the primordial state of Divine Pleasure in the Garden of Eden.

The word *Ru'ach* also means 'breath.' The inner wisdom of this month guides us to pause and breathe when we find we are not relating to external objects, such as food, with presence and purpose. Taking a slow and mindful breath before or in the midst of a physical pleasure allows us to bring our higher consciousness into our earthly experience. (We will continue to explore the importance of breath in greater detail throughout the second half of this text.)

TORAH PORTIONS

I N SHEVAT, THE *Parshios* / TORAH PORTIONS THAT WE READ include *Va'era* through *Yisro*. These Parshios take us through the story of the Exodus from Egypt, culminating in the receiving of the Torah on Mount Sinai — where the nourishing water of Torah is 'poured' into us (*Baba Kama*, 17a). Moshe, whose name means 'to draw,' was himself drawn from the Nile by Pharaoh's daughter after his parents had faithfully placed him in a basket in the river to evade the Egyptian decree to kill all first-born Israelite sons. Additionally, before the Exodus, Moshe draws water for the daughters of Yisro (*Shemos*, 2:19). Ultimately, he himself becomes the ultimate embodiment of the *D'li*, the great 'water pourer' or transmitter of Torah wisdom to the world.

In the beginning of Shevat, the Torah portions also speak of the Ten Plagues, which, as mentioned, are connected to the Divine *Sheivet* / rod of justice, alluding to the dominant energy of *Din* present in the first half of Shevat.

In the weekly portion of Yisro, the Torah was revealed on Mount Sinai. Yisro is the name of Moshe's Midianite father-in-law, known to be a most influential spiritual leader of the pagan world. The name Yisro comes from the root word *Yeser* / addition. Yisro was the first *Ger* / convert added to the Jewish People, and in a sense, he expanded the Torah to include converts. Our Sages say that he added an entire *Parsha* to the Torah, and this was named after him in honor of his *Chidushim* / innovative additions to the Torah. Yisro's new ideas on delegating leadership responsibilities were accepted by Moshe and became an integral part of the Torah. So too, when our *Chidushim* are aligned with the revelation that was received at Mount Sinai, we can expand the reach of the Torah into new areas of life and thought. This is another example of the concept of expanding Kedusha / holiness into new realms explored earlier in relation to the Torah verse connected with the month of Shevat. Those who were born in Shevat, under the influence of the *Mazal* / sign of *D'li* / Aquarius, tend toward originality in thought; this gift can be used to create innovative applications of Torah wisdom.

As we learned, through the Tribe of Asher, Shevat is also connected with oil. Oil is associated with *Chochmah* / wisdom, as our Sages say, "Whoever is accustomed to use oil merits *Chochmah*" (*Menachos*, 85a). Chochmah represents the kernel of an idea, the seminal drop of insight that enters one's consciousness in a concentrated manner, like a drop of oil. When oil is lit, it can produce abundant light and illumination.

More specifically, Shevat is associated with the *Chochmah* of *Malchus*, which is the wisdom of speech and communication. This is illustrated by the communication of the Torah through Moshe. Moshe redeems speech for the entire people of Israel, as the exile of Egypt was an exile of speech (*Zohar 2*, 25b). Moshe, too, suffered initially from a constriction of speech. After the Giving of the Torah, Moshe was healed of his speech impediment and he became a man of words (*Zohar 2*, p. 25a; *Agrah DePerkah*, 166; *Medrash Raba*, ibid). Throughout the Torah portions of Shevat, Moshe is transformed from a person who was *Kvad Peh* / heavy of mouth and unable to communicate, into the great mouthpiece and channel of Divine speech. From then on, the Torah says regarding *Hashem's* revelations to the people of Israel: "These are the words of Moshe" (*Devarim*, 1:1).

Chochmah of *Malchus* was also embodied by *Serach*, the daughter of *Asher* (the archetypal tribe of Shevat). When Serach was a young girl, she communicated to Yaakov that his son Yoseph, whom he thought was killed many years prior, was still alive. She did so in a gentle way, allowing Yaakov to receive the news without an overwhelming shock, which would have traumatized him. In this extremely delicate moment, she was able to communicate with such tenderness because, like Moshe, she personified the wisdom of communication. Her words "revived Yaakov's spirit," helping to transform the *Din* of his life into *Chesed*.

This month, we, too, can tap into the wisdom of speech by communicating powerful Torah to others in a sensitive manner, and speaking in such a way that we revive the spirits of people around us.

These teachings indicate that the month of Shevat is ultimately concerned with both what goes into and comes out of our mouth, whether it is food or speech. On a deeper level, what and how we eat has the power to purify our speech, as eating represents our primal physical appetites and reveals the state of our soul through the actions of our body.

SEASON OF THE YEAR

*A*S MENTIONED PREVIOUSLY, SHEVAT IS TECHNI-CALLY a winter month, but it is also understood as being a time of transition between the depths of winter and the hidden stirrings of spring. In the Land of Israel, the Sages teach us that during the month of Shevat, after a long winter period of dormancy, the sap begins to flow in the trees again. What has been in hibernation and held in reserve due to the cold of winter is roused afresh during the month of Shevat, returning a sense of vitality to the natural world. We, too, experience this sub-tle shift — especially if we take the time to tap into and appreciate it. This is one of the main purposes of Tu b'Shevat: *to sensitize us to what is happening in the world around us and to help us realize that, as "a human is like a tree," the same dynamic shifts are occurring within us as well.*

This particular seasonal dynamic also has an impact on our relation to food and eating. When the weather is hot, people tend to eat less; this is one reason why many people tend to lose weight in the summer. In the winter months, people are more inclined to enjoy food in abundance, as their bodies seek to bulk up to keep warm. When it is very cold, however, in the depth of winter, it is more difficult to enjoy one's food. At this time, it is basically too cold to enjoy anything. Our systems, in a certain sense, power down and pull on reserves during the dead of winter. Teves, which is the month before Shevat, is the coldest month of the year. When Shevat comes, the intensity of the cold begins to subside. During this period, when it is cold but not bitterly cold, people start to focus on food again. Life begins to return. The sap begins to flow. Spring, and all the vibrancy and physicality it entails, is on its way. Because of this, the Sages instituted the fasts of *ShoVaViYM* as a means to gain mastery over our eating habits and to create a Tikkun for our relationship to food in general. Shevat is a perfect time to work on our physical appetites as we prepare for the inevitable abundance and temptations of the approaching warmer months.

We will now explore and expand many of the basic concepts developed above within the context of Tu b'Shevat, the signature holiday of the month of Shevat.

THE HOLIDAY OF THE MONTH:

Tu b'Shevat
New Year of the Trees

*T*HE HOLIDAY THAT OCCUR THROUGHOUT THE YEAR should be understood as specific times set aside for each of us to experience and put into practice the theoretical and spiritual teachings of the Torah related to each month as revealed by the Sages. This form of amplified experience is akin to a kind of spiritual "practice" in which we seek to develop a specific skill or capacity within a given time frame. The particular skill or capacity that we develop within the ritual context of a specific holiday is then obviously meant to be integrated into the rest of our life on a daily basis. For instance, we are not meant to only access joy on Purim or liberation during Pesach. These are qualities that inform and inspire our lives throughout the calendar year. Each holiday is thus a special time for us to deepen our ability to access the unique attributes represented within the particular holidays for the betterment of our life as a whole.

TU B'SHEVAT
New Year of the Trees

*T*HE TRANSLATION OF THE WORD SHEVAT AS A 'ROD OF JUDGMENT' alludes to a Day of Judgment or *Rosh haShanah* of sorts. Specifically, Tu b'Shevat is the "*Rosh haShanah* of the (Fruit) Tree" (*Rosh haShanah,* 1:1). Nevertheless, according to some of our Sages the actual Judgment Day for trees may occur much earlier in the year, perhaps on Sukkos, or even on *Rosh haShanah* proper (*Rosh haShanah,* 16a). In what sense then is Tu b'Shevat considered a new beginning for the trees, and what does this have to do with us?

Furthermore, *Rosh haShanah* proper, which occurs on the first of Tishrei, is typically thought of as the birthday of the world or of humanity. So what does it mean that there are multiple "New Years," so to speak? And how do these different New Year's observances relate to one another?

In the Talmud, there is a discussion about whether the world/humanity was created in the fall on the first of Tishrei (*Rosh Ha-Shanah*) or in the spring on the first of Nisan. According to the deeper teachings (*Tosefos, Rosh haShanah,* 27a), these two positions are not mutually exclusive. In the fall, on the first of Tishrei the *idea* of humanity was *conceived*; in the spring, on the first of Nisan the *actual* world/human was *born*. Essentially, these dates are two paradigmatic points in the developmental process of impregnation, gestation, and birth of a seed-idea on its way to becoming an actual tree or fruit (i.e., world/human). But what does this have to do with Tu b'Shevat? Let's go deeper.

In the cycle of the year, Tu b'Shevat, the 15th day of Shevat, is exactly opposite Tu b'Av, the 15th day of the summer month of Av. Tu b'Av is 40 days before the 25th of Elul, which is considered Day One of Creation — the birthday of the world. *Rosh haShanah,* which occurs five days later, thus celebrates the creation of Adam and Chavah (i.e., humanity) on the first day of the month of Tishrei — considered the Sixth Day of Creation. Tu b'Av, which is the ancient holiday when single Israelite men and women would go out to the field to find their soul-mates, is thus 40 days before the "conception" of the seed-idea of creating the world and humanity, which occurred on the 25th of Elul. Tu b'Av thus represents the *falling in love* and *building of desire* phase that precedes the "conception" of creation, metaphorically speaking.

Following this thread, we find that Tu b'Shevat is 40 days before the 25th of Adar, which parallels the 25th of Elul, when the seed-idea of the world was planted within Hashem's fertile mind and heart, so to speak. Tu b'Shevat is thus 40 days before the world and humanity were actually born. This represents the time when the idea starts to feel real, when parents say to themselves: "This is actually happening! We better get prepared!" In short, Tu b'Shevat is the time when we prepare for the inevitable emergence of a new physical reality and the demands it places upon us. In psycho-seasonal terms, this refers to the rebirth of nature that occurs in spring, which correspondingly presents us with many new joys and challenges; one of which is how we will interact with all the new bounty and beauty that will blossom in the near future. Tu b'Shevat provides us with an opportunity to focus on rectifying and re-balancing our relationship to food specifically, and our physical appetites in general.

Tu b'Shevat thus empowers us to expand Kedusha and spirituality into the physical dimensions of our lives. This day revives us from the dead of winter, and blesses us with the chance for a new beginning at the decisive fulcrum of our lives: the primal act of eating.

☾

THE TIKKUN OF EATING
& HOW TO EAT MINDFULLY

As mentioned previously, there are many reasons that people eat beyond satisfying their physical hunger. There are people who eat for taste — and even when not actually hungry, they will eat tasty foods. There are others who eat in order to socialize, as eating with others creates a certain level of social bonding. Some eat out of boredom, as the act of preparing, procuring, and eating food temporarily alleviates this feeling. There are those who tend to binge-eat when they feel lonely in an attempt to soothe themselves. Others are inclined to eat for no reason when they feel tired or depressed — especially sweet foods, since a high sugar content can create a temporary feeling of stimulation or uplift.

Another ulterior motivation to eat is to gain a sense of groundedness, security, or solidity. This desire can arise when one feels anxious or unstable, but also when 'returning to the world' after an intense spiritual experience, such as immersion in prayer. It is also natural after intense physical exercise to need nutritional replenishment and perhaps to desire heavier foods. Additionally, 'grounding' might be sought through food after physical intimacy, prolonged mental focus, or a highly emotional experience.

The Baal Shem Tov speaks of a person who prays with great depth, has a real experience of mystical unity, and then seeks to settle down by drinking alcohol. However, one can learn to anchor and ground their 'higher' experiences in more direct and productive ways. For instance, after an intense physical, emotional, mental, or spiritual experience, we can effectively ground ourselves by performing a good deed or Mitzvah. This action will have the same 'anchoring' effect of eating, but will serve the dual purpose of feeding our souls as well as potentially benefiting others besides ourselves. The practical wisdom of when to eat, and why, is a fundamental lesson we all must learn in the process of balancing, healing, and rectifying our body, mind, and soul.

As quoted earlier: "The *Tzadik* eats to satisfy the soul; but the belly of the *Rasha* is always empty" (*Mishlei*, 13:25). When we eat for reasons other than satisfying the actual needs of the body, we ultimately feel just as empty, bored, lonely, depressed, or ungrounded as when we started eating. These feelings of need may even be exacerbated; and on top of that, we will feel stuffed and heavy. The Tzadik on the other hand, the person who eats with attention and intention, will ultimately gain satisfaction from their food.

Tu b'Shevat empowers us to create a great Tikkun upon all our eating throughout the entire year. Our eating from then on has the potential to reach the level of Adam and Chavah before their spiritual descent (*Pri Tzadik, Beshalach*).

EATING ON A HIGHER/
DEEPER LEVEL:

Tu b'Shevat is the "*Rosh haShanah* of the *Ilan* (singular) Tree." Why is it called the "New Year of the Tree" and not "of the Trees?" The deeper reason behind this linguistic clue is that it hints to "*the* Tree," the Tree of Life in the Garden of Eden. On Tu b'Shevat we have the ability to create a Tikkun for all eating done in the realm of the Tree of Knowledge and to eat again from the Tree of Life.

The numerical value of *Ilan* is 91 (*Aleph*/1 + *Yud*/10 + *Lamed*/30 + *Nun*/50 = 91), the same numeric value of Hashem (*Yud*/10 + *Hei*/5 + *Vav*/6 + *Hei*/5 = 26) plus *Ado-noi* (*Aleph*/1 + *Dalet*/4 + *Nun*/50 + *Yud*/10 = 65); 26 + 65 = 91. The name Hashem represents the Transcendent aspect of the Divine, and the name *Ado-noi* represents the Immanent aspect of the divine. *Ado-noi*, which is the name we pronounce instead of Hashem, is thought of as the manifest vessel that contains the infinite energy and potential of Hashem in this world. The perfect relationship to the fruit of an *Ilan* is one in which there is a unity between the actual food (represented by the name *Ado-noi*) and the consciousness of the eater (represented by the name *Hashem*). This is the idea of mindful and deliberate eating with holy intention and purpose. This unity of spiritual and physical worlds, between consciousness and consumption, is the paradigmatic goal of Tu b'Shevat.

Achilah, the Hebrew word for the act of eating, represents an action in the realm of the physical world. In fact, the name *Ado-*

noi has the same numeric value (adding 1 for the word itself) as the word Achilah, 66 (Arizal, *Sha'ar haMitzvos, Parshas Eikev*). As mentioned, the Name *Ado-noi* represents Divine Immanence, the manifest presence of Hashem in this physical world. Thus, when a person eats with Kavanah / intentionality, he creates a unity between Hashem, the Transcendent aspect of G-d, and *Ado-noi,* the Immanent aspect of G-d.

In Hebrew, when a food is prepared to be eaten it is called a *Ma'achal.* The numerical value of *Ma'achal* (*Mem*/40 + *Aleph*/1 + *Chaf* /20 + *Lamed*/30) is also 91. When we spiritually prepare ourselves to eat, and then eat with Kavanah and without haste, we are creating a unity between Hashem and *Ado-noi*, between the spiritual intention and the physical action. We are infusing our utilitarian, animal-like activity with deeper and higher purpose.

Eating when one is bored, depressed, or lonely are all forms of mindless eating. Eating without being physically hungry, but just because the food is placed in front of you, or eating too quickly, are also forms of mindless eating. When Adam and Chavah were told that they could eat from all the trees of the Garden, just not from the Tree of Knowledge, this prohibition was only in place until the onset of Shabbos. Adam and Chavah were created, and a Divine soul was breathed into them, on Friday. They were then told not to eat from the Tree of Knowledge until Shabbos, which represents the Tree of Life paradigm within the dimension of time. Once Shabbos had begun, says the Arizal, they would have been allowed to eat from the Tree of Knowledge, but they lacked patience. They were not able to wait until Shabbos and they ate from the Tree of Knowledge on Friday, which led to their expulsion from the Garden.

On another level, as will be explored more in depth shortly, there was only ever one tree, and its identity, as either the Tree of Knowledge or the Tree of Life, was ultimately dependent upon how and when Adam and Chava ate from it. Had they waited until Shabbos and eaten its fruit in holiness, they would have been eating from the Tree of Life, but because they ate the fruit mindlessly and impatiently, they transformed the Tree of Life into the Tree of Knowledge. The quality of consciousness that we bring to our eating determines whether we are eating from the Tree of Death and Duality or the Tree of Living Unity.

Eating from and identifying with the Tree of Knowledge paradigm thus represents impulsive eating, shoveling food down one's mouth without thought or Kavanah. This is mindless, purposeless eating, such as eating in order to keep busy or to be distracted. We can, thankfully, create a Tikkun on these careless ways of eating. By rectifying our relationship to the fruits that we eat on Tu b'Shevat, we are rectifying our relationship with the Tree itself. On Tu b'Shevat we inspire a spiritual elevation and expansion of the parameters of *Kedusha* into the physical world by eating fruits slowly, patiently, and mindfully — with focused attention and intention. This level of eating on Tu b'Shevat opens up a channel for spiritual energy to flow into our lives, which then irrigates our eating throughout the rest of the year. This Divine flow is the "river that issued out of Eden to water the Garden" (*Bereishis*, 2:10).

THE FOUR PATHS OF EATING

As we have determined that the primary focus of the month of Shevat and of the holiday of Tu b'Shevat is to rectify our eating, and thereby expand the realm of holiness to embrace the physical world, we will now dive into these ideas a bit deeper. To clarify these issues a little more, we will explore four different ways of relating to food, which are also four ascending levels of approaching life in general:

1) Indulgence, 2) Avoidance, 3) Equanimity, and 4) Holy Re-engagement.

1) Indulgence. To impulsively indulge in food is The Way of Unconscious Action. This represents our tendencies toward addictive, impulsive, and mindless eating. We are called upon by the Torah and the Sages to evolve and refine these tendencies.

2) Avoidance. The first stage of breaking a psychological dependency on food is to refrain from selfish indulgence. This may include fasting completely, avoiding certain foods, or decisively separating oneself from over-indulging. This is The Way of Self-Rectification, corresponding to the classic teachings of *Mussar*. Fasting can be practiced for a day, or even for a few hours, such as skipping breakfast. Fasting can also be done while in the midst of eating. *Rabbeinu Yonah* (Spain, 1200- 1263), the great moralist and Tzadik, suggests that if you find yourself indulging in self-centered eating or getting overwhelmed by your appetite, put down the food and stop eating for a moment (*Yesod haTeshuvah*). Creating a mini fast while in the middle of eating can mean pausing until the next meal, or even just pausing for a few moments to re-center yourself. In truth, it is much deeper (and harder) to refrain from eating while in the midst of eating than to simply fast (*Yesod haAvodah* [*Slonim*], p. 148d). Either way, the goal is to extricate yourself from mindless dependency on external stimuli.

3) Equanimity. The path of avoidance is a reaction to unconscious indulgence, and therefore it is in itself a form of inverted indulgence. There is a third way that can open up to us once we have learned to refrain: *Hishtavus* / equanimity. This is The Way of Transcendence, corresponding to the teachings of *Kabbalah*. The Kabbalist *Rabbi Yitzchak of Acco* (1250-1340) teaches that we should aspire to reach a spiritual plateau where we are always 'equal,' level-headed and balanced before all events and experiences. Someone who has established this level is unaffected by the praise or blame of others (*Meiras Einayim, Ekev,* 11:18. See also *Chovos haLevavos, Sha'ar haK'nia* 7 and *Sha'ar Yichud haMa'aseh* 5. *Magid Mesharim, Beshalach.* R. *Chayim Vital, Sha'arei Kedusha,* 3:4). This practice of equanimity can be applied to eating, to the point that all qualities and quantities of food are realized to be psycho-spiritually equal and satisfying, even if they are physically or sensually distinct (*Tzav'as haRiVaSh,* 2).

4) Holy Re-engagement. The highest or deepest path is *b'Chol Derachecha Da'eihu* / Know Hashem in all your ways — to sense and know the Divine pleasure within the physical pleasure of eating. This level represents holy enjoyment beyond equanimity. This holy pleasure is the blissful recognition of the Divine Essence within everything. It is The Way of Essence, corresponding to the path of the Baal Shem Tov, called *Chassidus*.

Along these lines, the Zohar (*Beshalach*) speaks of *Klal Yisrael* leaving Egypt and being freed from the work and mentality of slavery — and says that this brought them to a higher mode of eating.

According to the Zohar, there are four types of eating and relating to food: a) eating as a slave, represented by *Mitzrayim* / Egypt; b) eating as a free person, represented by *Matzah* / unleavened bread; c) eating as an angel, represented by the *Mon* / Manna, which is similar to a young infant suckling; and d) the eating of a *Talmid Chacham* / a wise student of Torah, characterized by a sense of *Mochin d'Gadlus* / expansive consciousness.

Selfish indulgence is the level of 'eating like a slave.' Refraining from indulgence is the first level of 'freedom from slavery,' and angelic equanimity is a higher level of freedom. Holy pleasure or 're-engagement' is complete freedom of being, which only a human with free-will and determination can attain.

We will now explore each of these stages in greater depth.

SLAVE EATING

Eating like a slave implies relating to food from a place of physical, mental, emotional, and spiritual constriction. *Mitzrayim* / Egypt, which is related to the linguistic root meaning 'constriction' or 'narrowness,' represents a confinement and limitation of consciousness, thought, speech, and behavior. With regards to eating, Mitzrayim signifies addiction and unhealthy attachments. Your thoughts, words, and actions are unconsciously attached to and ruled by the image of food and your anxious expectations of self-gratification.

Put simply: if when you wake up each morning you must drink coffee in order to function and feel well, then you are enslaved to coffee. If there are certain foods you *must* eat, or certain times of day when you must fill your belly, or else you will be off-kilter or emotionally reactive, this suggests that you are living in some level of dependency or 'slavery.' This is called *Yeshus* / egoic existence and helpless attachment to form. In such a state, whether you know it or not, your soul is yearning to be free.

FREE-PERSON EATING

A more liberated way of eating and living is represented by Matzah / the Bread of Freedom. The Israelites ate Matzah as they left Egypt and their previous state of slavery. What is it about Matzah that embodies the quality of freedom?

A slave is someone whose life is dependent upon and fused with his master or his external surroundings. A free person is independent and autonomous. If, in order to consider yourself intelligent, you need someone else to tell you how smart you are, you are enslaved to other people's opinions. If you are not dependent on anything or anyone in order to survive and thrive, you are, in a sense, free.

Matzah symbolizes and expresses this freedom. It is a very simple food, as it contains only the most essential ingredients of flour and water, and is baked in the shortest time possible. Simplicity is freedom. Matzah is completely simple and free from other influences and qualities. It does not depend on external additives such as sugar, salt, oil, or a long baking process. It is free of extraneous ingredients and free of time. It is what it is, rather than existing for an ulterior purpose.

Eating on the level of freedom is eating from a place of *Ayin* / no-thing-ness. Practically speaking, this means that you do not really care how your food tastes, feels, or looks; these externalities are nothing to you. This is just like Matzah, which has a relatively bland taste, appearance, and texture. On this level, your only goals in eating are nutritional nourishment or Mitzvah-fulfillment. There is a measure of *Hishtavus* / equanimity in this indifference to the external qualities of your food.

More accurately, this level of *Ayin* / no-thing-ness or detachment is really the *Ayin* of the *Yesh* / the no-thing-ness of something, or the emptiness of form. Practically speaking, if you need to detach from something, it means that you are still attached to it; it still exerts influence over you on some level.

On this level of eating you do not want to be stuck to the *Yesh* of food — to its form, taste, texture, color, volume, or vitality — so you detach yourself from these dimensions of eating. You choose to interact with food from the place of *Ayin*. In this way food is nullified before you, so to speak.

If you break your attachment to drinking coffee by telling yourself: "I am no longer dependent on coffee to give me a good morning, so I will not drink coffee for a month" — this implies that you are indeed still attached to it. Coffee still potentially controls you. You would not need to avoid something if you were truly independent from it. If you fast from food as a way to transcend over-indulgence, it suggests that you are still connected to its indulgence, otherwise you would not have to create such impermeable boundaries. Even *Hishtavus* / equanimity can be connected to reactivity.

Klal Yisrael ate Matzah as they were running from Mitzrayim; it was thus an instrument for gaining freedom. Their only way to break free of enslavement was to run hastily out of Mitzrayim and everything it represented. This haste is the paradigm of Matzah, which is baked in haste so it doesn't become old and fermented.

When we feel addicted to something or someone, the first move must often be to hastily break out and run from the situation, to let go of the old fermenting attachments and refrain from indulging them anymore.

This is a necessary step toward freedom. Yet, it is still the *Ayin* of the *Yesh*, the dialectical opposite of the *Yesh*, not its fixing, elevation, and ultimate reintegration.

ANGELIC EATING:
EATING EVERYTHING
WITHOUT DESIRE

After Klal Yisrael finished eating the Matzah they brought with them out of Mitzrayim, Hashem gifted them with an even higher form of eating: the *Mon* / Manna. As we will see, *Mon* differs from Matzah in that Matzah has no real flavor. In the previous stage represented by Matzah, one is essentially avoiding the overwhelming world of flavors and textures in order to gain a sense of distance and balance over their appetite. On that level, the food has become *Ayin*, but not the person who eats the food. The next stage represented by *Mon* is the ability to eat and taste any kind of food without desire or attachment. This level is the full manifestation of *Ayin*-consciousness, as one now permits themselves to eat flavorful food again, but remains unattached. This stage is similar to being an infant nourished by his mother's bosom. *Mon* is often compared to breast-milk by the Sages for a variety of reasons that we will now explore.

Mon was a food that fell from Heaven. It is referred to by our Sages as "angel food" (*Yuma*, 75b), and although it had the nondescript appearance of a white seed, it tasted like whatever food the eater wished. It thus contained the potential for all tastes. The Torah says, "And the taste of it was like the taste of a cake baked with oil" (*Bamidbar*, 11:8). *Reb Avuha* said, "Do not read *L'shad* / cake, but *Shad* / bosom. Just as an infant finds many flavors in the breast, so also did *Klal Yisrael* find many tastes in the *Mon*" (*Yuma*, 75a). Indeed, mother's milk contains traces of various tastes from the foods the mother has eaten, and similarly the *Mon* contained every possible taste.

Mon is also intricately connected with Moshe. Just as the Well and the Pillars of Smoke and Fire accompanied the Israelites through the desert on account of Miriam and Aharon, the *Mon* manifested in the merit of Moshe (*Ta'anis*, 9a). Moshe is thus a conduit of the nurturing "mother's milk" of the *Mon*. While leading the Israelites through the desert Moshe says to Hashem that he feels like he is carrying *Klal Yisrael* as "a nursemaid carries a suckling child" (*Bamidbar* 11:12. "This verse is a statement, not a question." *Ohr haChayim*, ad loc). After we were birthed as a people through the Exodus, we were like infants nursing from the 'bosom' of Hashem via the nursemaid Moshe, as it were. It is understood that all of *Klal Yisrael* were in a state of *Yenikah* / suckling during their journey through the desert (*Sha'ar haKavanos, Derush Pesach,* 1), and their source of spiritual and physical nourishment came to them through Moshe. In fact, when other Israelites prophesied in the desert, they too had names related to bosom, such as in *El-Dad* / to the bosom, and *Mey'dad* / from the bosom (see *Mishnas Chassidim, haChalav,* 1:1. There are right/*Chesed* and left/*Gevurah* sides of the bosom. In general, Moshe became the great transmitter of Torah because of the purity of his own 'nursing.' *Sotah,* 12b. *Maharsha,* ad loc.)

Although the *Mon* contains any and all tastes, it is really *Ayin*, as it contains 'nothing' prior to human projection. It is absent of all inherent context and form, and is only an expression of the pure potential of all tastes. As mentioned, the *Mon* is described as being like a seed; one reason for this is that it is the seed of all tastes.

Moshe, too, represents the level of *Ayin*, as he lives in the place of *Ayin* / nothingness, and complete humility. In the context of food, this state represents the absence of all physical desires and attachments to taste. In the desert, Klal Yisrael ask Moshe for meat, which symbolizes desire: "Who can give us flesh to eat? ... Now our soul is dried away, there is nothing at all; we have nothing but this *Mon* to look at" (*Bamidbar,* 11:4-6). Moshe responds, *"Me'ayin Li Basar* / From where can I produce meat?" (*Ibid,* 13) — but his words can also mean, "I am *Ayin*, so how can meat (desire) come through me?"

Moshe is *Me'ayin* / of *Ayin*; he is rooted in the paradigm of *Ayin*, the unitive emptiness and potency prior to form. An illustration of this is found deep within his name. The three letters in Moshe are

Mem, Shin, Hei. Mem is spelled *Mem-Mem* (the additional letter when thus 'filled' is *Mem*). *Shin* is spelled *Shin, Yud, Nun* (the added filling letters are *Yud* and *Nun*). Hei is spelled *Hei* and *Aleph* (the filling letter is *Aleph*). All of these filling letters — Mem, Yud, Nun and Aleph — can be arranged to spell the word *Me'ayin* (R. *Menachem Tziyoni, v'Zos haBeracha*. Also cited by the *Shaloh, Shemos*, 2).

In this episode, Klal Yisrael thus comes to Moshe and says: "we want desire, re-attachment to form. Yes, we have *Mon* and it tastes like anything we want, but we want to have desire itself; we want meat, flesh. Our souls are dried away," they say, "and we are tired of seeing seeds — the spiritual seeds of taste — day in and day out." Although the *Mon* tasted like meat, still they complain: *Vayisavu Ta'avah* / a desire they desired (*Bamidbar*, 11:4). A deeper reading of these words suggests: They desired to have desire. They wanted to want. On the surface, this may seem like a weakness or lapse of spiritual station on the part of the Israelites; but as we will see shortly, this *desire to desire* is actually a positive response to angelic equanimity, which is not the end-goal of this developmental process.

Humans are not meant to be angels. We are not meant to be so detached from Hashem's creation that we cannot connect to it or be moved by it. Truly, all creation contains a trace of the Creator, and as Hashem glories in the depth and beauty of His creation, so should we. Ultimately, the desire to desire is what propels us forward to attain our full and rectified humanity. However, this takes discipline and mindfulness so we do not get lost in the quicksand of the physical world. It is only from a place of holy reintegration that we are able to connect with and elevate the hidden sparks of spirituality contained within all creation.

As mentioned, on the level of *Mon* there is no *Ta'avah* / desire. They tasted within the *Mon* almost any type of food and delicacy. They certainly tasted various types of meat, yet they still wanted meat itself; they wanted to regain a sense of physicality after eating only Matzah and *Mon*. A newborn infant lives in complete humility and without specific desires. But later, as he grows, the mother's milk that is available to him day in and day out starts losing its appeal — no matter how nourishing. When something is always available to you, you start losing a desire for it. A yearning for solid foods arises in the child, along with a desire for the will to be independent from his mother — and thus, he complains.

Additionally, the *Mon* had all the "tastes and textures" of what they desired (*Yuma*, 75a), but it lacked a corresponding visual appeal: "We are tired of seeing seeds." Whether it tasted like meat or cake, it still looked the same, and so they lost desire for it. "The eyes see and the heart craves" (*Rashi, Bamidbar*, 15:39). This means that the heart only truly desires what the eyes see (*Sotah*, 8a); *Ta'avah* comes from the eyes. And thus, the absence of visual stimulation caused them to stop experiencing desire and real satisfaction until they realized that what they really desired was to have desire once again, but on a higher/holier level than they initially had as slaves in Mitzrayim (*Yumah*, 74b).

This higher level of desire, which we will explore more fully in the next section, is what pushes the Israelites (i.e., us) out of the spiritual "no-man's-land" of the wilderness and into the Promised Land of Israel. Entry into Eretz Yisrael signifies a return to form, function, and physicality — but on a deeper and higher level than we had access to when we were slaves in Mitzrayim. The goal of leaving Mitzrayim and wandering through the desert to enter into Israel is to deconstruct our unconscious attachments and addictions, and to develop conscious control of our physical appetites and spiritual abilities.

On the angelic level of equanimous eating, we can eat anything with little or no desire. We are no longer slaves to our food; we are not attached and do not over-indulge. When we relate to food with little or no desire, we can eat anything but we are not totally controlled by it. We are not utterly absorbed in the taste of our food to the level of addiction. Nor have we given up and let go of all sense of taste in this angelic state of equanimity, rather we can connect to the taste — but without the inner disturbance of mindless craving. All foods are like the *Mon* to us; we taste everything we wish to taste, while at the same time we are like a newborn — simply content to be merged within its mother's presence.

On this level, we are starting to re-engage with food without the need for strict avoidance. We are free, but not yet on the highest level of freedom, which includes desire, but in a rectified and elevated manner. At this stage, we are still like an angel whose will is nullified and merged with the Divine will; but this is not the ultimate goal, which is the attainment of our full humanity, as represented by the archetype of the *Chacham* / the Wise One.

Remember, as mentioned at the beginning of this book: *Equanimity is the foundation of pure and holy pleasure*; but it is not the highest level of human perfection, which is the re-integration of holy desire within the spiritual context of Torah beyond mere detachment or disinterest. This, as we will learn, is the deeper meaning of Shabbos.

☾

SOUL EATING:
EATING EVERYTHING
WITH HOLY DESIRE

Souls are beyond angels, and the ultimate objective is to eat on the level of souls — also known as the level of a Tzadik / righteous enlightened person, or *Talmid Chacham* / a student of Hashem transformed by Divine wisdom. This dynamic state of consciousness is represented by the Israelite's entry into Eretz Yisrael and is defined by the quality of *Mochin* / Mind; hence the terms mindful and mindfulness. An individual living at such a level is the opposite of mindless or careless with his or her actions and appetites.

As we mentioned above, "The Tzadik eats to satisfy his soul" (*Mishlei*, 13:25), and as the Zohar interprets, "the Tzadik is already satisfied before he even eats." In other words, the Tzadik eats from a place of wholeness and satisfaction, and not from a place of *Cheser* / lack or incompleteness. He does not eat to fill an emotional hole, whether it is loneliness, depression, anxiety, or a general feeling of emptiness. He eats when his body is genuinely hungry, not when his spirit or psyche is lacking. From this place of spiritual fullness, he is able to eat to the point of physical fullness and satisfaction.

Mochin-filled or mindful people feel full, whole, and complete, without the need for anything outside of themselves to fill them. Thus, they eat for the sake of the nutrients and the life-force in the food that keeps the body alive, healthy, and happy. Yet, this is not a merely utilitarian approach to food. The Divine will and perspective is that we should live and thrive in health and joy; this includes permissible pleasures experienced to the extent of our rectified and holy desire.

If what you truly seek is to connect to and experience Divine pleasure, if all you want is to lose yourself and be one with Hashem, then you will begin to feel this same Divine pleasure within every pleasure in Hashem's world. In this way, the realm of the spirit is expanded to embrace the physical world, as discussed previously regarding the Torah verse connected with the month of Shevat.

A Tzadik, the *Talmid Chacham*, is so attached to the Creator's perspective of reality, so unified with *Hashem*, that he comes to know the boundless Divine beauty and pleasure existing within everything in Hashem's Creation. This is experiencing the world from the perspective of *Yesh Amiti* / true existence. This state of being allows one to access holy pleasure, which is the experience of the Divine Essence within everything.

Here's how to get a glimpse of holy pleasure: Put this book down for a minute and pick up an apple or any other fruit in your hand.

Pause for several seconds and settle your mind. Take a deep look and appreciate the profound beauty and intricate detail of the fruit; take a deep inhale and allow the scent of the fruit to fill your nostrils; then, draw the awareness of Hashem down into the act of eating by reciting a meaningful blessing with intention and passion. Now take a bite and feel the fullness of Hashem's glory extending all the way into the tastes and textures you are experiencing. When you eat this way, the total fullness and essence of your *Yesh* / self becomes one, as it were, with the Divine spark within the fruit. You may even feel the taste of the fruit down to your very toes.

If your entire being is in a state of *Ta'anug* / pleasure, you are connecting to the purpose of your very creation. As the Ramchal, a profound Italian mystic/philosopher from the early 18th century, writes: "Man was created for the sole purpose of rejoicing in Hashem and deriving pleasure from the splendor of His presence; for this is true joy and the greatest pleasure that can be found" (*Mesilas Yesharim*, 1. See also *Alter Rebbe, Likutei Torah, Balak*, 71a). When you experience the *Ta'anug* of *Hashem*, which is the ecstatic pleasure of being consciously absorbed within the Divine Unity, then you will sense pleasure throughout your entire body and within everything you are experiencing.

This is the deepest way of living — seeing and experiencing the full deliciousness of Hashem's light sparkling within every moment and within every-thing. This is the path that the holy Baal Shem Tov revealed to the world.

A wise Chassidic Rebbe, *Reb Simcha Bunim of Pshischah*, once scoffed at those who sang the praises of their spiritual master, claiming that he was so spiritual that he did not even taste the food that he ate. "A real Rebbe," replied *Reb Simcha*, "is one who truly and deeply tastes his food. As it is through such enjoyment that one is able to taste the Divinity within everything that he eats and experiences."

To review: 'Slave eating' comes from a state of *Yesh* / egoic existence, and is represented by *Mitzrayim*. 'Free person eating' is without attachment, corresponds to Matzah, and comes from a preliminary state of *Ayin*-consciousness (the *Ayin* of the *Yesh*). Eating and tasting everything but without any desire is an angelic level, corresponding to *Mon*, and comes from fully established *Ayin*-consciousness. Beyond all of these three levels is eating on the level of the *Neshamah* / soul, which corresponds to *Mochin*, is represented by *Eretz Yisrael*, and comes from the paradigm of *Yesh Amiti* / True Existence, or Ultimate Oneness. We thus begin in a state of unconscious *Yesh (Mitzrayim)*, move through various states of *Ayin (Matzah* then *Mon)*, until we are able to re-engage and re-integrate into the world of *Yesh*, but on a deeper and higher level than we started from *(Mochin)*. In summary, the stages develop in this order: *Mitzrayim, Matzah, Mon, Mochin.*

REALITY AS UTILITY
OR PLEASURE

To pleasure in Hashem's presence in every moment and in every-thing is to live in the paradigm of the Tree of Life — the essence of Gan Eden.

A closer reading of the Torah reveals that the Tree of Life is a reality saturated with holy pleasure, and our correct participation within that world is primarily to humbly and gratefully receive Divine pleasure. The Tree of Knowledge reality, by contrast, is utilitarian in nature, and is based in the self-serving and greedy attempt to grab more and more.

"And Hashem planted a garden eastward in Eden; and there he put the man whom he had formed. And out of the ground Hashem made grow every tree that is *Nechmad* / pleasant to the sight, and *Tov* / good for food — the Tree of Life in the midst of the garden, and the Tree of the Knowledge of Good and Evil" (*Bereishis*, 2:8-9). Here, "Pleasant to the sight," the element of aesthetic pleasure, precedes and is dominant over "good for food."

Later, when Chavah is about to eat from the Tree of Knowledge it says, "And she saw that it was *Tov* / good for food, and *Nechmad* / pleasurable to the eyes" (*Bereishis*, 3:6). The order is reversed from the original sequence. Here, Chavah is relating to the world as an 'it,' an object to be consumed; from this vantage point, the world is primarily "good for eating." This utilitarian and self-centered perspective asks, "What can I get from the world and from other people?" Ego has become the prism through which Chavah sees everything. This shift in perspective is ultimately what led to the eating from the Tree of Knowledge.

❦

ONE TREE

From this deeper perspective, we can understand that the Tree of Life and the Tree of Knowledge are really one and the same tree. They each respectively represent two different ways that we can relate to the single Tree of Reality. Similar to the Quantum conundrum of "Schrödinger's Cat," in which a theoretical cat behind a closed door is potentially both alive and dead until one opens the door to reveal its actual condition, at which point it can be only alive or dead, the single Tree of Reality contains the co-existent potential of both the Tree of Life and the Tree of Knowledge. However, once a person acts or 'eats' from the single Tree of Reality, similar to opening the door in the example above, the fruit of their action will reveal itself to be from either the Tree of Life or the Tree of Knowledge, depending on how and why the 'fruit' was 'eaten.'

The Torah says with regards to the Tree of Life and the Tree of Knowledge: "…the Tree of Life in the midst of the garden, and the Tree of the Knowledge of Good and Evil" (*Bereishis*, 2:9). Thus, we know that the Tree of Life is in the "midst of the garden," but where is the Tree of Knowledge?

A location for the Tree of Knowledge is not specified because both the Tree of Life and the Tree of Knowledge are "in the midst of the garden"; they have the *same location*. In other words, they are the very same tree (*Pri Tzadik, Beshalach*). Another way of saying this is: The essence of all trees — 'tree' being a metaphor for all reality — contains both the Tree of Life and the Tree of Knowledge. The Tree of Knowledge is just a particular relationship that a person has with the Tree of Reality.

This begs the question: How do we relate to Life? Adam and Chavah, and we as well, are given a choice to eat, or relate to experience, from either a Tree of Life or a Tree of Knowledge perspective. To "eat from the Tree of Life" is to internalize the Oneness of Life, the *Achdus* Hashem / unity of Hashem within our own lives. Whenever we relate to the Divine Oneness through the prism of our world, we are tasting from the Tree of Life. To "eat from the Tree of the Knowledge of Good and Evil" is to internalize the apparent duality, separation, disconnection, and conflict in life. A tension between good and bad appears, which itself feels bad. Whenever we see things from this perspective, or give energy to this perspective, we are eating from the Tree of Duality. Whatever we taste and internalize is what we identify as, and this determines our output to others and to the world, as well.

"And out of the ground Hashem made every tree grow that is pleasant to the sight, and good for food, the Tree of Life in the midst of the garden, and the Tree of Knowledge…" It follows that the two descriptions, "pleasant to the eyes" and "good for food" refer to the Tree of Life paradigm and the Tree of Knowledge paradigm, respectively. The world of the Tree of Life, of *Achdus* / unity is "pleasant"; it is Divinely beautiful and pleasurable. It is an aesthetic world, so-to-speak. The world of the Tree of Knowledge, of separation, is "good for food"; it is a utilitarian world. "Every tree" means that the paradigm of Divine pleasure and the paradigm of utilitarian struggle are potentially found within each and every tree in the Garden of Life.

Gan Eden, in general, represents the Tree of Life paradigm. Within Gan Eden, the deepest level of living, grows the Tree of Life of holy pleasure. In the Tree of Knowledge paradigm, on the other hand, consciousness functions on a superficial level and therefore lacks real pleasure. Before Adam and Chavah ate from any tree, they saw their lives as primarily pleasurable and beautiful. However, as soon as Chavah moved toward eating, internalizing, and identifying with the Tree of Knowledge, she first observed that the Tree was "good for food" — good as separate from bad. She had a shift in consciousness into calculative thinking: seeing things primarily for their worldly utility and payoff, rather than for their potential to express Divine presence and pleasure.

WEEKDAY IS GOOD
SHABBOS IS PLEASURE

The Vilna Gaon (*Ideres Eliyahu*) points out that the word *Tov* / good, as in "good for food," is found in the Torah with regard to each of the Six Days of Creation. Even though Day Two is not explicitly described by the word *Tov*, in Day Three the word *Tov* appears twice, once for Day Two and once for Day Three. The only day of Creation where the word *Tov* does not appear at all is Shabbos, the Seventh Day.

This means that the weekday, the work-week or mundane reality, is intimately connected to the utilitarian perspective of *Tov* — whereas Shabbos is beyond the quality of *Tov* / good, it is *Nechmad* / pleasurable. Shabbos is a time of pleasure and delight (*Yeshayahu*, 58:13), a time of *Ta'anug*. On Shabbos there is an elevation of all the *Tov* of the week to the level of *Nechmad*. This dynamic is illustrated beautifully in *Gematria*: the word *Tov* is numerically 17. Six days of *Tov* (6 x 17) equal 102, which is the numerical value of the word *Nechmad*.

During the week, we are connected with the world of utility, the Tree of Knowledge; whereas on Shabbos we are connected with pleasure, the deeper reality of Gan Eden and the Tree of Life. As we step back from our weekday activities of constructive creativity, we have more space and time to appreciate the inherent radiance and beauty of Hashem's creation in all of its aspects. The world then transforms before our very eyes from being a finite deposit of raw materials for our further manipulation, into a unified creation that is complete within itself. During the week, we act as artisans, perpetually tweaking and tinkering with the world's constitutive elements. On Shabbos, we shift into the role of the audience with front-row seats at the multi-sensory symphony of Hashem's creation; the world, in all of its dimensions, becomes a work of art that contains the hidden signature of the Ultimate Artist, Hashem. This dynamic of the world being manifest as either Tov during the week or Nechmad on Shabbos, mirrors the dual potential of the single Tree of Reality, the fruit of which can manifest as either the Tree of Life or the Tree of Knowledge, depending on how and why we eat it.

"Hashem planted a Garden *b'Eden* / in Eden" (*Bereishis*, 2:8). *B'Eden* means *in* Eden, but then the question becomes — "where is Eden?" Eden can also mean pleasure. Therefore, "planted a Garden *b'Eden*" means that Hashem planted the Garden within the dimension of Divine pleasure (*Kesav u'Kabalah*, ad loc).

In the highest, deepest form of pure pleasure, there is no consumption or elimination of the vehicle of that pleasure; rather, one loses oneself and becomes fully absorbed within the Divine essence permeating that object. Receiving pleasure from a beautiful sight, sound, or taste does not diminish, eliminate or 'kill' its spiritual energy or potential. On the contrary, from the Tree of Life paradigm, aesthetic pleasure is a vitalizing and necessary ingredient in the full-spectrum experience of the fullness of Hashem's glory.

By contrast, the Tree of Knowledge brings with it "death." Hashem says, "Of the Tree of the Knowledge of Good and Evil you shall not eat, for on the day that you eat thereof, you shall surely die" (*Bereishis*, 2:17). The obvious question is: What does this mean, seeing that they did not die on that day, but rather went on to live long lives?

"You will surely die" means, 'by eating from the Tree of Knowledge you will become mortal and thus *eventually* die.' When they ate from the Tree of Knowledge, they suddenly and for the first time became painfully aware of their mortality.

Furthermore, following Adam and Chava's eating from the Tree of Duality, all eating took on the quality of death in some respect. Whereas previously, there was no duality perceived between life and death, as all of life was related to as one unified process; now after having eaten the fruit from the Tree of Duality, it was understood that for us to eat, something first has to die, whether animals or fruits. In fact, the Hebrew word for the act of eating, *Achilah*, comes from the same word as *Kilayon*, which means expiring or ending. Following the sin of eating from the Tree of Knowledge, we feed off of death, and so does the entire ecosystem. In essence: life feeds off death.

There is also a subtler reading of this verse: By eating from the Tree of Knowledge and entering the world of duality and separation, everything they subsequently ate required some process of elimination of waste. From then on, everything they internalized eventually had to die or be separated from them again. As such, the body rejects and expels the used or dead nutrients as waste. Thus, death has become intermingled with the life-giving aspect of food.

In fact, human feces contain dead red blood cells that need to pass from the body. Every time we eat, we are engaging with subtle forms of death — especially when our eating is unhealthy; or, in a case of constipation, when toxic waste and dead cells are separated within the body but not properly released out of the body.

It is interesting to note that the feces of an infant are not *Halachically* considered as feces *(Shulchan Aruch, Orach Chayim, Siman* 81). Spiritually speaking, that is because infants do not live in a world of *Pirud* / separation, and so they do not experience death in eating. They still live in a Tree of Life world. Similarly, before eating from the Tree of Knowledge, the food of Adam and Chavah was like the *Mon* in the Desert, the "food of angels," and therefore produced no waste. That is, the *Mon* was "absorbed by all the two hundred and forty-eight parts of the body and no refuse was left" (*Yuma,* 74b). The food remained alive in them, and unified with them. This is a hint at the way we eat and process food on Shabbos.

Ultimately, on the level of consciousness, the real death is the separation of one's sustenance from the Source of Life. When one does not view their food as having come from Hashem, the Wellspring of All Blessing, there is an element of death, or finite energy inherent within it. When one perceives their food as the physical manifestation of G-d's spiritual bounty, then there is an aspect of the infinite within every bite.

EATING FROM THE TREE OF KNOWLEDGE ON SHABBOS

As explained above, the deepest way of eating is not the way of "angel food," but the way of "soul food." Soul food is pleasurable, but not merely like the *Mon*, which did not have a stimulating visual beauty or aesthetic element. The full experience of absorbing, internalizing, seeing, eating, and sensing the Divine pleasure within every morsel of food is an experience of unity and duality simultaneously — it is the fruit of the Tree of Knowledge eaten within the realm of the Tree of Life, as one tree.

As previously mentioned, the Arizal teaches that the original intention of the Creator was for Adam and Chavah (i.e., us) to eat from the Tree of Knowledge, but just to wait until Shabbos. In other words, Hashem wanted Adam and Chavah to acknowledge duality and differentiation, but only within the total fullness of Hashem's glory. Shabbos is the paradigm of the Tree of Life. If they would have eaten from the Tree of Knowledge on Shabbos, they would have actively included the fullness of duality within the greater context of the Tree of Life paradigm of Unity and Divine pleasure. Instead, they internalized duality during the week, placing it in service of limited utility, which made it appear separate from the holistic context of Gan Eden consciousness. The glory and magnificence of duality-in-oneness was concealed, and thus they exiled themselves from their eternal life of Divine Pleasure in Paradise.

Indeed, we are designed to delight in eating and to behold the richness of every morsel of food — to sense within all its colors, tastes, and textures the *Kevod Hashem* / the fullness of Hashem's creative force. But in order to do that, we first need to identify with the Tree of Life, with Shabbos, with Hashem's unity; otherwise, we may get lost in self-centered utilitarian eating and unconsciously indulge in destructive cravings, thereby exiling ourselves from real satisfaction, which nourishes both body and soul.

☾

THE PATH OF THE BAAL SHEM TOV

Now let us return to our previous discussion of the four levels of eating: indulgence, avoidance, equanimity, and holy re-engagement. The first level, indulgence, is not really a "way of life," rather it is a danger and detriment to life. In other words, it is not a way that we choose, rather it is the default setting that determines our actions when we do not activate our free choice. The other three paths — avoidance, equanimity, and holy re-engagement, corresponding to the paths of *Mussar*, *Kabbalah*, and *Chassidus* / the way of the Baal Shem Tov — are appropriate choices for any person at different times, depending on their circumstances.

These paths also evolve from one level to the next. If we find ourselves dependent on indulgence, we may need to move to 'stage two' and fast or refrain from some or all food in some way. Once we are detached from our dependency, we can move to 'stage three' and re-engage with eating but from a place of equanimity, where all food is considered equal, whether tasty or bland. From a place of equanimity, we can then safely re-engage with reality and truly experience the holy pleasure and wonder of food with gusto and *Gadlus* / expansive consciousness. In fact, on this level we can re-introduce desire for specific flavors and textures, as at this stage our desire has been purified and elevated to the extent that our true desire is only for Hashem. Any desire we may have for a particular food would be understood at this level as only representing a particular garment of Hashem's essence, which is what we truly desire.

We must remember when considering and clarifying these different ascending levels of eating, that fasting or denying the needs of the body can be just as addictive and egocentric as over-indulging one's cravings. Similarly, pure equanimity can lead to dry indifference and stoicism. The path of the Baal Shem Tov, however, includes the beneficial elements of discipline and detachment while avoiding their pitfalls. This allows one to indulge in the Divine Pleasures of Hashem's creation in a way that is healthy, life-affirming, and inter-connected.

On the path of *Chassidus*, we can fast from the self-centered desire for taste, while simultaneously eating *and enjoying* sumptuous foods. Thus, we are not stuck in a mode of avoidance. We can simultaneously practice equanimity *and* taste the thrilling beauty of Hashem's presence. Thus, we are not stuck in a mode of indifference. In this path, we can eat like a Tzadik. Ultimately, this path can empower us to fix the mishap of Adam and Chava and transform the Tree of Knowledge back into the Tree of Life. This is also referred to as eating from the Tree of Knowledge on Shabbos.

☾

PLEASURE PERMEATING THE ENTIRE BODY

Prior to Adam and Chava's eating from the Tree of Duality, the earth was divinely instructed to bear trees where the fruit and the trees themselves — including the bark, trunk, branches, and leaves — all tasted equally delicious. Once Adam and Chavah ate from the Tree of Knowledge, there was a separation, which caused the tree and its fruit to taste differently: the fruit was edible, whereas the bark, for instance, was for the most part inedible (*Medrash Rabbah, Bereishis*, 5:9).

The tree itself represents the inner reality of a particular object or experience, and the fruit represents its outer manifestation. When the tree and the fruit taste the same this means that the outer and inner aspects are unified and in sync; this is the paradigm of the Tree of Life. When the tree and fruit do not taste the same, this is a paradigm of separation and duality, represented by the Tree of Knowledge.

The relationship between the tree and the fruit can also be understood as process- or product- oriented consciousness, or, as the paradigms of journey and destination orientation. The Tree of Life, in which the tree and the fruit are experienced as one, represents an awareness of the value and purpose of the whole process and journey of the seed. Whereas, the Tree of Knowledge, in which only the fruit is deemed valuable, represents a lack of appreciation for the whole process, and an over-valuing of the product or destination of the journey. This is what ultimately separates the fruit from the tree, and leads to the suffering and perceived curse of work — where one is only focused on the outcome of one's efforts rather than on the meaning and miracle of every step along the way.

In today's Tree of Knowledge reality, every pleasure that we receive comes to us through two constricting 'garments': 1) the physical, finite garment of the object of pleasure — the thing or person which is giving the pleasure; and 2) the physical, finite garment of the subject of pleasure — we who are receiving the pleasure (The *Leshem, Sefer haDe'ah* 2, *Derush* 4, 11:4).

When we taste a fruit, for example, it is only the flavors and physical qualities of the fruit that give us pleasure, and not any it's more subtle energetic aspects. In the Tree of Knowledge paradigm we do not procure pleasure from the entirety of the tree/fruit because its multi-dimensional wholeness is restricted and therefore not all of it is available to us. This is the limitation within the object of pleasure itself.

From a Tree of Knowledge perspective, the same restrictions are present within the recipient of the pleasure. When we eat a tasty fruit it is only with our taste buds and mouth that we sense the pleasure of taste, and not with the other parts of our body. This has been the case ever since Adam and Chavah ate from the Tree of Knowledge — the paradigm of restriction and separation. In the Messianic Era, however, we will eat from the Tree of Life — the paradigm of Unity. That means we will freely access pleasure without the intermediary of *Levushim* / garments or limitations within the object of pleasure or within ourselves. The essence and the entirety of a fruit will 'touch' the essence and entirety of our very being.

Experientially speaking, this means that our entire self, not just our taste buds or our stomach, will take pleasure from the entirety of the fruit and the totality of the tree. It will be a full-body experience; even our toes will sense the unmitigated pleasure of the full Divine glory present within the fruit.

This is perhaps the deeper reason why we eat fruit on Tu b'Shevat. The judgment of Tu b'Shevat is on the trees themselves, not on the fruit. The fruits are judged on Shavuos (*Rosh HaShanah*, 16a). And yet, we celebrate Tu b'Shevat by eating the fruit, and not by gaining pleasure from the tree itself, as in, carving a piece of wood, for example. Why? This is to show that on Tu b'Shevat we are beginning to make a Tikkun for the eating from the Tree of Knowledge by unifying the separation between tree and fruit. *On Tu b'Shevat we are, essentially, putting the fruit back onto the Tree of Life.*

On this level of eating, we experience *Hana'ah* / pleasure in the fullness of the deliciousness of the foods; and within these pleasures, we sense the fullness of Hashem's presence within the world. In fact, the Baal Shem Tov teaches that the very *Ta'am* / taste of the food (and its fragrance) is where the Divine animating force within the food is (most) present. The taste and fragrance of a fruit, for example, are not as tangible as the actual fruit itself; they are more *Ruchni* / spiritual, as they have no mass or weight. This is precisely where the *Chayus* / Divine life force within the fruit resides; and once ingested, this spiritualized life-force now nourishes and gives strength to the eater (*Ma'or Einayim, Emor*). For this reason, *Reb Simcha Bunim of Pshischah* once quipped: "Foods with no taste are fattier/heavier" (i.e.; they have more physical weight and less spiritual substance).

However, it is important to note that while we should certainly enjoy and experience a deep level of *Hana'ah* from the flavor of the foods we eat, as that is where the *Chayus* lies, we must also make sure that we are eating with more than just simple, bodily *Ta'avah* / desire. Our enjoyment of creation's physical fruits must remain connected to the Creator's spiritual roots.

While picking a beautiful apple, for example, we should not close off our senses so that that we receive no *Hana'ah* from the taste or fragrance of the apple. Rather, it is just the opposite: We should take a moment, breathe, hold the apple, feel its curves, see its colors, and recite a slow and Kavanah-filled *Beracha* / blessing before we bite into it and relish in its deliciousness. In this manner, we may ultimately enjoy and connect with the *Chayus* / Divine animating life-force within the apple and elevate our own eating for the sake of Unification.

Appropriately, along these same lines of thought, *Reb Mendel of Rimnov* once said that the Divine sparks that we liberate through eating are elevated specifically through the *Oneg* / pleasure that we experience while eating.

When we eat in this way, and are attuned to the deeper truth of the teaching to 'Know G-d in all your ways,' our eating becomes an expression of The Way of Essence. In this way, we are able to taste the Tree of Life even while eating common breakfast cereal. We are thereby able to expand the light of holy pleasure into the realm of physical food, and thus to make a *Tikkun* / rectification for the eating from the Tree of Separation.

There may seem to be an almost imperceptible difference between these higher and lower approaches to eating, and by extension, between the higher and lower experiences of any of life's gifts. To honestly know whether we are eating from the deepest place or simply fooling ourselves, we should emplace a temporary *Me'at* / diminishment in our involvement with *Ta'am* / taste in order to test and notice the effects of our eating on our body and mind. The words *Ta'am* and *Me'at* are composed from the same letters, revealing an inherent need for this periodic pausing and diminishment of consumption so that we can clarify our true motives. Are we really relishing in the Divine pleasure reflected within the world, and living from a place of *Ta'amu uRi'u Ki Tov Hashem* / tasting the goodness of Hashem? Or, are we just eating on the first level of self-centered indulgence? If, when we pause, we realize that our eating leads to tiredness or sleepiness, a sense of separation or muted awareness, then we can know for certain that we are stuck eating on the lower level of separation and self-centered indulgence. But, if our eating brings us positive *Koach* / strength and energy, then we may very well be connecting to the Divine Spark and Pleasure within our food — reflective of the higher levels of holy eating.

☾

FRUIT ON TU B'SHEVAT

The paradigm of the Tree of Life is especially apparent and accessible to us through fruit, and that is the deeper reason why we specifically eat fruit on Tu b'Shevat — as we are making a Tikkun on both our personal eating and on the primordial eating of the Tree of Knowledge. Historically speaking, fruit is a luxury item. Bread and water are considered staples for survival, while fruits are most often eaten for pleasure. As mentioned previously, this taste for the finer things is represented by the Tribe of Asher, who was blessed with and blesses us with abundance, richness, and pleasure — particularly in relation to food. A survival food is eaten because we are lacking something; we are hungry, deficient, or lacking in energy, and we need the food to complete us. This approach of 'completing what is lacking' is rooted in the paradigm of utility and separation. Yet when we eat fruit, for the most part, we do not eat it from a place of lack, but for pleasure and enjoyment, and so it more vividly represents the world of Unity, Pleasure, and the Tree of Life.

This is the deeper reason the Torah likens a human being to a tree (*Devarim*, 20:19), and to the fruit of a tree (*Tehillim*, 92:13. *Medrash Tehillim*, ad loc. *Chagigah*, 27a. *Shir Hashirim Rabbah*, 1:2. Whereas all other forms of life are likened to grass: *Kli Yakar*, *Bereishis*, 1:11). As the trees and their fruits were designed to provide various pleasures, we are designed to receive these very pleasures. This is also why originally, man ate only fruit: "Hashem said…of every *tree* of the garden you may freely eat" (*Bereishis*, 2:16). This verse suggests that initially only fruit, and not even vegetables, were permissible to be eaten. Fruit is thus an expression of our intrinsic bond with the Tree of Life represented by the reality of Adam and Chavah in their original state in Gan Eden.

☾

A NATION SATURATED WITH PLEASURE

During this month, may we be blessed and empowered to let go of our self-centered attachment to food — and to all external substances — and to actualize our capacity for Divine pleasure. On Tu b'Shevat, as we partake of delicious fruits and delicacies, may we taste the Divine Presence and expand the boundaries of Kedusha. May we radically realize that we are capable of expanding Kedusha into the realm of physical pleasure because the source of our souls is rooted in the Supernal *Ta'anug* / Divine pleasure (Noam Elimelech, Shemos). The Friday evening prayers refer to us as an *Am Medushnei Oneg* / a people saturated with delight and holy pleasure. Each of us is capable of this ecstatic delight, even amid our worldly needs and concerns.

On Tu b'Shevat we have the opportunity to realign the first two letters of the Divine Name and channel an abundant flow of kindness into the world, rather than the *Din* present during the first half of the month of Shevat, which is represented by the reversal of the order of the first two letters of Hashem's Name (as discussed previously). May we bring the day, when for all people, the pleasures of this world will be unified with the deepest, formless pleasure of knowing Hashem. As King David sings, "...*V'hisaneg el Hashem!* / take pleasure in the Infinite One! (*Tehillim*, 37:4).

SUMMARY OF SHEVAT

12 DIMENSIONS OF SHEVAT	
SEQUENCE OF *HASHEM'S* NAME	H-Y-V-H
TORAH VERSE	*Vayikra*, 27:33 — *Ha'mer Yemirenu V'ha-ya Hu...* 'If anyone makes a substitution, both the animal [and its substitute become holy.]'
LETTER	*Tzadi / Tzadik*
MONTH NAME	*Sheivet*, (rod or staff)
SENSE	*Le'itah* (taste)
ZODIAC	*D'li* (Pitcher, Aquarius)
TRIBE	*Asher*
BODY PART	*Kurkavan* (esophagus)
ELEMENT	*Avir* (air), or *Ru'ach* (wind)
PARSHIOS	*Va'era* through *Yisro*
SEASON	Winter
HOLIDAY	*Tu b' Shevat* (15th of *Shevat*)

ᕦ
SUMMARY

IN THE MONTH OF SHEVAT, OUR AWAKENING APPETITE during this stage of the Winter **season** calls upon us to make a Tikkun on our eating. The energy of the month empowers us to extend the presence of Kedusha into the physical realm of eating, and also of relating to objects in general. To receive this empowerment, we must practice interrupting and releasing our drive for instant gratification, mindlessness, and haste in order to make a *Tikkun* on the *Kurkavan* / esophagus or 'food pipe' (the **body part** of the month). In order to release this drive for instant gratification, it helps to pause before or during consumption in order to breathe deeply and calmly. Doing this connects us to the **element** of the month, *Ru'ach* / 'wind', making our mind and body more flexible like *Avir* / air, and more capable of clarity and mindfulness. In addition to pausing and breathing, we must harness our powers of *Le'itah* / taste, the **sense** of the month, and focus on tasting the Divinity within our food. These empowerments are especially available during this month's **holiday** of Tu b'Shevat, when we eat fruits with the intention of tasting the Creator's Presence within creation.

The **letter sequence of *Hashem's* Name** for this month begins with a backward flow (*Hey-Yud*), and ends with a forward flow (*Vav-Hei*). This points to a shift in energy from *Din* to *Chesed*, which occurs in the middle of the month during the holiday of Tu b'Shevat. The **name** of the month, which means *Sheivet* / staff, has similar import: the staff of Moshe, upon which the Four Letter Name was inscribed, channeled *Din* / Divine harshness when held upside down, and *Chesed* / Divine kindness when held right side up. The **Parshios** of this month dramatize this same narrative: through Moshe's leadership, the harshness of the Egyptian Exile is turned back upon itself and the *Chesed* of Redemption is revealed.

The **verse** that bears the letter sequence of Hashem's Name expresses the idea of expanding the territory of Kedusha in our lives. Expanding the territory of Kedusha is the function of a Tzadik; however, we can each participate in this activity as well, when we partake in the pleasures of life with mindfulness and holy intention. The **letter** of the month is *Tzadik* / a righteous, enlightened person — or *Tzadi* / hunt — both terms alluding to our spiritual mission to seek out and capture sparks of Kedusha within our food and any other objects or experiences that we encounter. The **sign** of the month, *D'li*, means 'to lift up,' as we are to bring these sparks of Kedusha together and elevate them, and also to pour them out for others in the form of enlightening Torah teachings.

The name of the **tribe** of the month, *Asher*, comes from the word *Osher* / joy or richness, and alludes to the *Sefirah* of *Keser*. These allusions guide us toward cultivating the ultimate state of *Ta'anug* / pleasure, the state attained by the Tzadik who consciously tastes the Divine Presence in all things. The following Kavanah / mindful intention is a step toward attaining this *Ta'anug*.

May we merit to harness the power of this month and train ourselves to taste the spark of Kedusha within every aspect of our lives.

FROM BREATHING TO BLESSING

As explored throughout this text, during the month of Shevat we need to reevaluate our relationship with food. We must ask ourselves during this time: Are we in control of our food or does our food control us? At the same time, we should examine our relationship to other external objects as well. Do we interact with anything in an unhealthy or unproductive way? Is the energy of addiction present anywhere in our lives? Contemplate whether or not you were able to pursue certain objects when you needed them, and whether or not you were able to let go of them when it was beneficial to do so. When you lost something, did you obsess about it? When something became old and worn, did you still hold on to it?

One simple method to help gain some mastery over our eating patterns is to learn to pause before and during eating. Every time you are about to begin eating, prior to taking a bite, take a moment or two to think about what you are about to do, and do not immediately push food into your mouth. Take a moment and consider whether you are eating because you are physically hungry, or whether you are eating to fill an emotional void.

Prior to taking your first bite of each category of food that you are eating, pause, become mindfully present and recite a *Beracha* / blessing with intentionality. The act of reciting a blessing provides you with the opportunity to recognize what you are about to do. A Beracha recited with proper intention opens you up to mindful presence and heartfelt gratitude in order to eat with a deeper purpose and connection to Divine pleasure.

If you said a Beracha before eating and now find yourself overeating or eating without presence of mind, pause again for a moment or two, as *Rabbeinu Yonah* suggests (as quoted above), refocus and then continue eating in a way that honors the Beracha. Whenever you feel the need — pause, breathe, and reset your focus. It would be worthwhile to actually make it a practice to periodically pause for a moment to refocus during every meal. In addition to helping you eat with more Kavanah / attention and intention, this practice will also ensure that you do not overeat.

Most of us should not eat until our stomachs are completely full, rather, we should try to eat at most three quarters of our fill (*Rambam, Hilchos De'os*, 4:2). Overeating is the root of many illnesses (*Hilchos De'os*, 4:15). By taking periodic mindful pauses as we eat, we ensure that we keep our digestive systems light, clean, and healthy. As discussed, only a true Tzadik should eat until they are physically full; that is because they were already spiritually full to begin with.

Conscientious and conscious eating creates a Tikkun for the

eating of the Tree of Knowledge. As we have mentioned, the Arizal writes that the prohibition to eat from the Tree of Knowledge was only temporary. The prohibition would have been lifted the moment Shabbos began. Yet Adam and Chavah were not able to wait, and this lack of patience was the source of their downfall. The first act of Tikkun for this impatience is to wait a little before we start eating, and to stop before we are completely full. The deeper and more difficult act is to pause while we are in the midst of eating in order to calm ourselves, refocus, and eat with presence and patience.

As we mentioned, the *Chush* / sense connected with Shevat is *Le'itah* / taste. The only place in the entire Torah that the etymological root of *Le'itah* (*L'hit*) appears is when *Eisav* hurriedly asks *Yaakov* to give him the lentil stew (*Even Ezra* on *Bereishis*, 25:30). This episode takes place right after the passing of their grandfather Avraham, and Yaakov is cooking lentils, which are a traditional food of mourning (*Medrash Rabbah, Bereishis*, 63:14). Eisav comes back hungry from his hunting spree and asks Yaakov for food. Yaakov agrees, on the condition that Eisav sell him the birthright of the firstborn child. Eisav responds, "Fine, who needs it? I am going to die anyway!" (*Bereishis*, 25:32). The way Eisav asks for the food is, "Pour into [me] some of this red, red (stew)" (*ibid*, 25:30). He then "opened his mouth like a camel and said, 'Pour it into my mouth!'" (*Medrash Rabbah, Bereishis*, 63:12). This represents unhealthy eating where one swallows his food mindlessly, in a rush, with no pause and sometimes without even chewing.

Eisav's eating is reminiscent of the eating of the Tree of Knowledge, when Adam and Chavah also exhibited impatience. Hashem tells them "…On the day that you eat thereof, you shall surely die" (*Bereishis*, 2:17). Thus, Eisav himself says during this episode: "I am going to die," and then gulps down the stew that Yaakov cooked in honor of Avraham's passing — a food connected to death and mourning.

Hurried, unsettled, and unhealthy eating creates an excess of waste and/or constipation, both of which correspond to death. Commit yourself, throughout this month, to ways of eating that bring life, peace, health and redemption to yourself and to the planet. Experiment with eating as a Tzadik or *Talmid Chacham* would eat, with *Mochin d'Gadlus* / expansive consciousness.

As mentioned, a *Talmid Chacham* is called Shabbos (*Zohar* 3, 29a). In other words, the *Talmid Chacham* is, in terms of *Nefesh* / consciousness, what the day of Shabbos is in terms of *Z'man* / time. When we eat on Shabbos, we are calm and joyful, and we enjoy tasting everything deeply. As a result of eating with holy desire and *Ta'anug*, we may produce little or no waste, just as the *Mon* produced no waste (*Pri Tzadik, Kedushas Shabbos, Maamar* 6). No matter the day, if we can access and enter into Shabbos consciousness, we can delight in the total fullness and beauty of Hashem's Creation. This Divine *Ta'anug* can spread into all the aspects of life, for within every enjoyment there is a gateway into holy *Ta'anug* and *Bitul* / self-nullification in the presence of the Divine.

During the Shabboses of this month, savor your food slowly, blissfully and gratefully. This month-long practice of mindful Shabbos eating will develop and strengthen your ability to eat with consciousness and composure throughout the rest of the year.

THE TWO PIPES

There are two 'pipes' that connect the head with the body: the *Kanah* / windpipe and the *Veshet* / food-pipe (the latter is another term for *Kurkavan* / esophagus, which is the body-part of the month). We damaged the *Veshet* by eating from the Tree of Knowledge. However the *Kanah* does not experience eating and drinking, and was therefore unaffected by the eating from the Tree of Knowledge. It is thus a *Bechinah* / an aspect of the paradigm of *Olam haBaa* / the World to Come, or the perfect wholeness that is coming into manifestation (*Shaloh, Sha'ar haOsyos, Oys Kuf, Kedushas haAchilah*, 232). *Olam haBaa* is a time or state in which *Ein Bo Achilah* / there is no need for eating (*Berachos*, 17a). This is connected to our higher self, our pure *Ruach* / spirit, which is rarely embodied in *Olam haZeh* / this world.

Veshet is thus an allusion to *Olam haZeh*, and *Kanah* is an allusion to *Olam haBaa*. The *Veshet* is precisely where the *Satan* / force of accusation and entrapment can gain a foothold. This is expressed in the fact that the words *Veshet* and *Satan* have the same letters, only that the *Vav* in *Veshet* is extended all the way downwards in the word *Satan*, becoming a Final *Nun*. The Final *Nun* represents a dramatic falling that occurs through reckless expansion, over-indulgence, and eating from the Tree of Knowledge (*Zohar* 3, p. 232a). In other words, when a person overeats, he expands the *Vav* of his *Veshet* into a *Nun* (*Shaloh*, ibid); and then, it can trap the flow of blessing and become a spiritual accuser, so-to-speak — an energy of the *Satan*.

To pause and breathe before we eat connects us to the element of the month, *Avir /* air. Mindful breathing is a shift into the *Kanah* paradigm, and this helps us to create a *Tikkun* for the fall of our *Veshet* into the forces of negativity. The *Yetzer haRa /* the personal tendency toward negativity and selfishness only entered into *Adam* and *Chava* after they ate from the Tree of Knowledge (*Rashi*, Bere-ishis, 2:17). The *Chet /* spiritual error was not that they ate from this Tree, it was that they ate from it impatiently; consuming it for pri-marily utilitarian purposes before Shabbos. As we learned, eating from this Tree on Shabbos would have been a positive, healthy act (*Arizal*, see *Ben Ish Chai, Bereishis, Halachos* Second Year). Thus, we need to learn to pause, wait, and breathe with our *Kanah*, so that we can eat with the *Veshet* in a healthy, positive way.

Reciting a blessing (or prayer), which is done with breath that becomes speech, connects us to the Higher World of *Kanah*, be-yond the World of the *Veshet* (*Pri Eitz Chayim, Sha'ar Yom Kippur*, 3). There is a simple transformation of the mouth that occurs when we recite a blessing before we eat. On one level, the gateway of all negativity and *Kelipa* (defined as receiving for the self and ego alone) is the mouth, as the mouth is an orifice of the body that 'takes in' from the outside and completely absorbs what it is taking in. Of course, we also breathe in air with our nose, hear with our ears, and absorb taste and touch with those senses respectively; yet, eating is the paradigmatic process of taking something completely separate from us and bringing it fully into our bodies so that it literally becomes us. Still, when we pause for a moment before we ingest, and use that very same mouth to recite a blessing of thanks-giving and gratitude to the Creator of all life, then the mouth of self-centered receiving is transformed into an instrument of praise.

And indeed, as our Sages teach: "The mouth was ultimately created to sing praises and thanksgiving" (*Shulchan Aruch Harav, Orach Chayim*, 60:4).

During the month of Shevat, we are empowered to undo and rectify all of the unhealthy eating and rushed swallowing of food that we did throughout the entire year. A good way to begin this Tikkun during this month is by training ourselves to pause and breathe (the World of *Kanah*) before we eat, in order to recite a blessing with real Kavanah. Additionally, it is beneficial to stop eating before we are completely full, as mentioned above.

RECITING A BERACHA WITH INTENTION

Joy and intention are essential for healthy and holy levels of eating. A person should accustom himself to eat with a joyous heart (The *Shaloh HaKodesh* quoting Rabbi *Yehoshua Ibn Shuaiv* (1280-1340), *Sha'ar HaOysyos, Kedushas Ha'achilah*). This is alluded to in the wise words of King *Shlomo* / Solomon: "Go, eat your bread joyfully and drink your wine with a merry heart" (*Koheles*, 9:7). Eating with joy and gratitude to Hashem for making these foods available for us to eat is healthy for both the body and the soul. Eating with joy and without tension or worry aids digestion, as well as helps to create the proper *Tikkun* for the eating from the Tree of Knowledge.

Once we achieve a level of gratitude and a joyful disposition, we can eat with more focus, mindfulness, intention, and attention. As we mentioned, an antidote to cure mindless eating and overeating is to pause and breathe every time we are about to eat something. Reciting a Beracha with intention and focus will certainly help us create a healthier relationship with food.

There is a state of the body that is called the acute stress response, also known as "fight-or-flight." When the body perceives danger, real or imagined, hormones like adrenalin and cortisol are released into the body, causing the heart rate to speed up and giving the body a burst of energy and strength. But what is most relevant to our conversation is that this response also slows down the digestive system, causing us to retain more calories by holding on to what has been eaten.

Sadly, we live in a world in which this stress response is activated many times throughout the day, even when neither fighting or fleeing is the appropriate response. This anxious state of being can be triggered from a variety of factors present in our sped-up and over-stimulated lifestyle such as stress at work, information overload, rush-hour traffic, and constant awareness of suffering, whether ours or others. The list goes on ad infinitum.

If we eat in this state of anxiety, we will eat quicker, we will eat more, and we will digest slower — leading to all kinds of stomach issues and weight problems. As explored earlier, when we connect merely with the physicality of the food, we are in danger of being controlled by our food, rather than the other way around.

And so, we need to ensure that when we sit down to eat, we are doing what we can to shift out of this overstressed mode of being in order to eat with a calmer, more relaxed, focused, and mindful state of being, with a 'joyous heart,' and with true gratitude. This is another wonderful reason why reciting a Beracha slowly and with Kavanah can have not just the obvious spiritual and psychological benefits, but also tangible physical benefits as well.

A Beracha said with proper attention and intention will certainly help us create a healthier relationship with food. Indeed, the words of the Beracha can be used as a profound meditation and entry into eating with holy purpose and pleasure.

The next time you are about to take a drink to quench your thirst, take hold of the cup, gather in your presence, focus your intention, and begin the blessing. Pause and breathe before reciting every one, two, or at the maximum three words. Think about the words you are about to utter as you inhale, and then, in one big exhale, recite each one, two or three words. Then think about the next one, two, or three words, as you inhale. And then with one big exhale, recite the next one, two, or three words.

When the words of the blessing are actually spoken, let go of your mental intentions and enter completely into the words and letters — try to feel the energy and vibration of the sounds of the words filling and infusing you. Have intention in the inhale and open yourself to visceral sensation when you are saying the word or words in the exhale. Repeat this rhythm until you conclude the blessing. The following is an extended Kavanah on the deeper meaning of the Beracha recited before drinking water.

☾

ॐ
PRACTICE:
From Breathing to Blessing
Reciting a Beracha with Intention

(Before reciting the words of the Beracha below, think to yourself:)

You Hashem are the Source of All Blessings.

I acknowledge this reality and desire this truth to be present in my life in a tangible way.

I want to be an open channel and make a revealed connection with You to draw down a stream of blessings into my life and into the world.

I desire a direct connection with "YOU," beyond all Names —

YOU the Transcendent, Infinite One!

Recite the blessing:

Baruch Atah Ado-noi
You are the Source of All Blessings, *Hashem*

(Before reciting the next word of the Beracha, think to yourself:)

...Who is not merely Infinite and Transcendent, but is tangibly revealed to us within the myriad details of our finite lives, in such a way that we can feel and call out to You as "Our personal and intimate G-d!"

Elo-hei-nu
Our G-d

(Before reciting the next words of the Beracha, think to yourself:)

...Who is not only *"our* G-d" but also the Master of the entire universe, faithfully present even within all the concealments of creation.

Looking at this cup of water, I may not be able to see the Divine animating force that enlivens and sustains the water, but that is only because the Light is concealed from my state of consciousness; yet I know and acknowledge that *Atah* / You, *Ado-noi* / Infinite One, *Elo-hei-nu* / our G-d, are fully present in my personal life and in the Life of All Worlds — as the caring Sovereign actively involved in every phenomenon and facet of Your Creation

Melech ha'Olam
Master of the Universe

(Before reciting the next word of the Beracha, think to yourself:)

Because everything,
literally everything,
including this cup of water...

(Then Recite:)

Shehakol
Everything

(Before reciting the next word, think to yourself:)

...Came to be and is coming to be in this present moment...

Nehiyah
Came to be

(Before reciting the next word, think:)

...Through Your Holy Speech.

The YOU who simultaneously manifests as Transcendent Power, as Indwelling Presence, and as Universal Sovereign, creates all Reality through Divine thought and vibration manifesting as speech; and it is this metaphysical vibration that is G-d's word that gives rise to all physical existence.

Bi-devaro
through His word.

(Think to yourself before taking a drink:)

When I am holding this small cup of water in my hands, I am holding everything that made this wonderful nourishing drink —

from the highest Source of All Blessing down to the molecular structure of H_2O.

Through this blessing, I have followed the flow of Divine energy from the utterly Transcendent Realm all the way down to the immediate physical reality, recognizing Hashem's You-ness and the Infinites One's presence at every step along the way— manifesting in this small cup of water.

I hereby acknowledge that: "Not by bread alone does man live, but by the word of Hashem."

Now take a drink and feel the presence and the majesty of the Creator within creation.

ॐ

IN CONCLUSION

"*Rav Chizkiah*...said in the name of *Rav*: In the Future one will be judged for all that his eyes saw but that he didn't eat" (*Yerushalmi, Kidushin*, 4:12). Indeed, it is a Mitzvah for a person to seek out and eat new fruits in order to be able to offer praise and thanks to Hashem and to show that we appreciate all the wonderful things that Hashem creates for us to enjoy in this world (*Mishna Berura, Siman* 225:19).

During the month of Shevat, and specifically on the holiday of Tu B'Shevat, we have the ability to sensitize ourselves to the majesty of the Creator within the fullness of life. As a result of this awareness we have the chance to deepen our appreciation and gratitude for all of life's pleasures and beauty, which are ultimately just vehicles for Hashem's presence in this world. Pausing and reciting a heartfelt blessing with Kavanah before eating is one highly effective way to help us achieve this wonderful state of being in constant wonder and amazement at the infinite awesomeness of the Creator and His beautiful creation.

Certainly there are more elaborate and esoteric practices prescribed by the Sages and Tzaddikim of past generations to help one evolve and expand their consciousness in relation to food and physicality, but it is not wise for one to dive into the deep-end without first learning how to swim. Additionally, it is always worthwhile to revisit the foundations of one's spiritual practice. It is often the simplest and most basic practices that yield the most abundant and profound results. There is always room to grow, and no one has fully drained the living waters of the wellspring of Hashem's blessing.

OTHER BOOKS BY THE AUTHOR

RECLAIMING THE SELF
The Way of Teshuvah

Teshuvah is one of the great gifts of life. It speaks of a hope for a better today and empowers us to choose a brighter tomorrow. But what exactly is Teshuvah? How does it work? How can we undo our past and how do we deal with guilt? And what is healthy regret without eroding our self-esteem? In this fascinating and empowering book, the path for genuine transformation and a way to include all of our past in the powerful moment of the now, is explored and demonstrated.

THE MYSTERY OF KADDISH
Understanding the Mourner's Kaddish

The Mystery of Kaddish is an in-depth exploration into the Mourner's Prayer. Throughout Jewish history, there have been many rites and rituals associated with loss and mourning, yet none have prevailed quite like the Mourner's Kaddish Prayer, which has become the definitive ritual of mourning. The book explores the source of this prayer and deconstructs the meaning to better understand the grieving process and how the Kaddish prayer supports and uplifts the bereaved through their own personal journey to healing.

UPSHERNISH: THE FIRST HAIRCUT
Exploring the Laws, Customs & Meanings
of a Boy's First Haircut

What is the meaning of Upsherin, the traditional celebration of a boy's first haircut at the age of three? Why is a boy's hair allowed to grow freely for his first three years? What is the deeper import of hair in all its lengths and varieties? What is the meaning of hair coverings? Includes a guide to conducting an Upsherin ceremony.

A BOND FOR ETERNITY
Understanding the Bris Milah

What is the Bris Milah – the covenant of circumcision? What does it represent, symbolize and signify? This book provides an in depth and sensitive review of this fundamental Mitzvah. In this little masterpiece of wisdom – profound yet accessible —the deeper meaning of this essential rite of passage and its eternal link to the Jewish people, is revealed and explored.

REINCARNATION AND JUDAISM
The Journey of the Soul

A fascinating analysis of the concept of Gilgul / Reincarnation. Dipping into the fountain of ancient wisdom and modern understanding, this book addresses and answers such basic questions as: What is reincarnation? Why does it occur? And how does it affect us personally?

――――――

INNER RHYTHMS
The Kabbalah of MUSIC

Exploring the inner dimension of sound and music, and particularly, how music permeates all aspects of life. The topics range from Deveikus/Unity and Yichudim/Unifications, to the more personal issues, such as Simcha/Happiness and Marirus/ sadness.

――――――

MEDITATION AND JUDAISM
Exploring the Jewish Meditative Paths

A comprehensive work encompassing the entire spectrum of Jewish thought, from the sages of the Talmud and the early Kabbalists to the modern philosophers and Chassidic masters. This book is both a scholarly, in-depth study of meditative practices, and a practical, easy to follow guide for any person interested in meditating the Jewish way.

TOWARD THE INFINITE

A book focusing exclusively on the Chassidic approach to meditation known as Hisbonenus. Encompassing the entire meditative experience, it takes the reader on a comprehensive and engaging journey through this unique practice. The book explores the various states of consciousness that a person encounters in the course of the meditation, beginning at a level of extreme self-awareness and concluding with a state of total non-awareness.

THIRTY – TWO GATES OF WISDOM
Awakening through Kabbalah

Kabbalah holds the secrets to a path of conscious awareness. In this compact book, 32 key concepts of Kabbalah are explored and their value in opening the gates of perception are demonstrated.

THE PURIM READER
The Holiday of Purim Explored

With a Persian name, a masquerade dress code and a woman as the heroine, Purim is certainly unusual amongst the Jewish holidays. Most people are very familiar with the costumes, Megilah and revelry, but are mystified by their significance. This book offers a glimpse into the hidden world of Purim, uncovering these mysteries and offering a deeper understanding of this unique holiday.

EIGHT LIGHTS
8 Meditations for Chanukah

What is the meaning and message of Chanukah? What is the spiritual significance of the Lights of the Menorah? What are the Lights telling us? What is the deeper dimension of the Dreidel? Rav Pinson, with his trademark deep learning and spiritual sensitivity guides us through eight meditations relating to the Lights of the Menorah, the eight days of Chanukah, and a fascinating exploration of the symbolism and structure of the Dreidel. Includes a detailed how-to guide for lighting the Chanukah Menorah.

THE IYYUN HAGADAH
An Introduction to the Haggadah

In this beautifully written introduction to Passover and the Haggadah, we are guided through the major themes of Passover and the Seder night. This slim text, addresses the important questions, such as: What is the big deal of Chametz? What are we trying to achieve through conducting a Seder? What's with all that stuff on the Seder Plate? And most importantly, how is this all related to freedom?

PASSPORT TO KABBALAH
A Journey of Inner Transformation

Life is a journey full of ups and downs, inside-outs, and unexpected detours. There are times when we think we know exactly where we want to be headed, and other times when we are so lost we don't even know where we are. This slim book provides readers with a passport of sorts to help them through any obstacles along their path of self-refinement, reflection, and self-transformation.

THE FOUR SPECIES
The Symbolism of the Lulav & Esrog

The Four Species have inspired countless commentaries and

traditions and intrigued scholars and mystics alike. In this little masterpiece of wisdom both profound and practical - the deep symbolic roots and nature of the Four Species are explored. The Na'anuim, or ritual of the Lulav movement, is meticulously detailed and Kavanos,, are offered for use with the practice. Includes an illustrated guide to the Lulav Movements.

––––––––––

THE BOOK OF LIFE AFTER LIFE

What is a soul? What happens to us after we physically die?

What is consciousness, and can it survive without a physical brain?

Can we remember our past lives?

Do near-death experiences prove immortality?

What is Gan Eden? Resurrection?

Exploring the possibility of surviving death, the near-death experience and a glimpse into what awaits us after this life.

(This book is an updated and expanded version of the book; Jewish Wisdom of the Afterlife)

––––––––––

THE GARDEN OF PARADOX:
The Essence of Non - Dual Kabbalah

This book is a Primer on the Essential Philosophy of Kabbalah presented as a series of 3 conversations, revealing the mysteries of Creator, Creation and Consciousness. With three representational students, embodying respectively, the philosopher, the activist and the mystic, the book, tackles the larger questions of life. Who is G-d? Who am I? Why do I exist? What is my purpose in this life? Written in clear and concise prose, the text, gently guides the reader towards making sense of life's paradoxes and living meaningfully.

BREATHING & QUIETING THE MIND

Achieving a sense of self-mastery and inner freedom demands that we gain a measure of hegemony over our thoughts. We learn to choose out thoughts so that we are not at the mercy of whatever belches up to the mind. Through quieting the mind and conscious breathing we can slow the onrush of anxious, scattered thinking and come to a deeper awareness of the interconnectedness of all of life.

Source texts are included in translation, with how-to-guides for the various practices.

VISUALIZATION AND IMAGERY:
Harnessing the Power of our Mind's Eye

We assume that what we see with our eyes is absolute. Yet,

beyond our ability to choose what we see, we have the ability to choose how we see. This directly translates into how we experience life. In a world saturated with visual imagery, our senses are continuously assaulted with Kelipa/empty/fantasy imagery that we would not necessarily choose. These images can negatively affect our relationship with ourselves, with the world around us, and with the Divine. This volume seeks to show us how we can alter that which we observe through harnessing the power of our mind's eye, the inner sanctum of our imagination. We thus create a new way to see and experience the world. This book teaches us how to utilize visualization and imagery as a way to develop our spiritual sensitivity and higher intuition, and ultimately achieve Deveikus/Unity with Hashem.

THE POWER OF CHOICE:
A Practical Guide to Conscious Living

It is the essential premise of this book that we hold the key to unlock many of the gates that seem closed to us and keep us from living our fullest life. That key we all hold is the power to choose. The Power of Choice is the primary tool that we have at our disposal to impact the world and effect change within our own lives. We often give up this power to outside forces such as the market, media, politicians or peer pressure; or to internal forces that often function beyond our conscious control such as ego, anger, lust, greed or jealousy. Making conscious, compassionate and creative decisions is the cornerstone of living a mature and meaningful life.

MYSTIC TALES FROM THE EMEK HAMELECH

Mystic Tales of the Emek HaMelech, is a wondrous and inspiring collection of stories culled from the Emek HaMelech. Emek HaMelech, from which these stories have been taken, (as well as its author) is a bit of a mystery. But like all good mysteries, it is one worth investigating. In this spirit the present volume is being offered to the general public in the merit and memory of its saintly author, as well as in the hopes of introducing a vital voice of deeper Torah teaching and tradition to a contemporary English speaking audience

INNER WORLDS OF JEWISH PRAYER
A Guide to Develop and Deepen the Prayer Experience

While much attention has been paid to the poetry, history, theology and contextual meaning of the prayers, the intention of this work is to provide a guide to finding meaning and effecting transformation through the prayer experience itself.

Explore: *What happens when we pray? *How do we enter the mind-state of prayer? *Learning to incorporate the body into the prayers. *Discover techniques to enhance and deepen prayer and make it a transformative experience.

This empowering and inspiring text, demonstrates how through proper mindset, preparation and dedication, the experience of prayer can be deeply transformative and ultimately, life-altering.

———————

THE SPIRAL OF TIME:
A 12 Part Series on the Months of the Year.

Now Available!

THE SPIRAL OF TIME:
Unraveling the Yearly Cycle

Many centuries ago, the Sages of Israel were the foremost authority in the fields of both astronomical calculation and astrological wisdom, including the deeper interpretations of the cycles and seasons. Over time, this wisdom became hidden within the esoteric teachings of the Torah, and as a result was known only to students and scholars of the deepest depths of the tradition. More recently, the great teachers, from R. Yitzchak Luria (the Arizal) to the Baal Shem Tov, taught that as the world approaches the Era of Redemption, it is a Mitzvah / spiritual obligation to broadly reveal this wisdom.

"The Spiral of Time" is volume 1 is a series of 12 books, and serves as an introductory book to the basic concepts and nature of the Hebrew calendar and explores the special day of Rosh Chodesh.

WRAPPED IN MAJESTY
Tefillin - Exploring the Mystery

Tefillin, the black boxes and leather straps that are worn during prayer, are curiously powerful and mysterious. Within the inky black boxes lie untold secrets. In this profound, passionate and thought-provoking text, the multi-dimensional perspectives of Tefillin are explored and revealed. Magically weaving together all levels of Torah including the Peshat (literal observation), to Remez (allegorical), to Derush, (homiletic), to Sod (hidden) into one beautiful tapestry. Inspirational and instructive, Wrapped in Majesty: Tefillin, will make putting on the Tefillin more meaningful and inspiring.

Printed in the USA
CPSIA information can be obtained
at www.ICGtesting.com
LVHW022041221223
767144LV00005B/87